May Batt.

19.9.41.

1   HURRICANES OVER FRANCE

FIGHTER
PILOT

A PERSONAL RECORD OF THE
CAMPAIGN IN FRANCE

September 8th, 1939, to June 13th, 1940

LONDON

B. T. BATSFORD LTD.

15 North Audley Street, W.1

First Published September 1941

MADE AND PRINTED IN GREAT BRITAIN FOR THE PUBLISHERS,
B. T. BATSFORD LTD., LONDON, BY THE TONBRIDGE PRINTERS LTD.,
TONBRIDGE

TO MY COMRADES
KILLED IN ACTION IN
THE BATTLE OF FRANCE

PUBLISHERS' PREFACE

THE author of this book is a Flight-Lieutenant in the R.A.F., now once again on active service at a Fighter Station in Southern England. His narrative took form from a series of daily diary notes recorded throughout the French campaign, which were " written up " periodically, when time allowed, in a fat copybook. This manuscript totals over 100,000 words, but contains much material of a personal nature that he has naturally not wished to appear in print. In fact, the earlier pages of the book, dealing with the months of comparative inaction prior to May 10th, 1940, represent only a few extracts from a very detailed account of his life and experiences at that time. From May 10th onwards, however, the narrative is printed almost exactly as it was written—which was not, it may perhaps be stressed, with any idea of publication in mind. To preserve its first-hand quality as a " personal record," both he and the publishers have thought it better that little further polishing or embellishment should be attempted.

As regards the illustrations, Figs. 1, 3, 4, 5, 6, 7, 8, 15, 16, 20, 22, 23, 24 and 25 are reproduced from British Official War Photographs, by kind permission of the Ministry of Information; Fig. 26 is from a photograph by the London News Agency; and Figs. 2, 9, 10, 11, 12, 13, 14, 17, 18, 19 and 21 are from photographs taken by the Author during the French Campaign.

2 DAWN AT VASSINCOURT

3   PRESS PHOTOGRAPHER'S VIEW OF No. 1 SQUADRON
(*Left to Right* : Billy, Leslie, Lorry, Prosser, Boy, the Bull, Moses, Johnny, the Doc.,
Paul, Killy, Stratters and Pussy)

4   LORRY AND LESLIE

FIGHTER PILOT

THE first week of war at Tangmere was too tense to be pleasant. We were waiting to go overseas with the Field Force, but there was no news day after day, and our time was spent between standing-by our aircraft and going up at each alarm. We were expecting to be bombed at any moment, but no bombers came, and soon the tension gave way to a feeling of unreality. It was difficult to realize that we were at war at all, and that men were dying in thousands on the Polish frontiers, while all was so peaceful here. The sun shone just the same, the windmill on the hill looked just the same, the fields and woods and country lanes were just the same. But in the background of our minds was a feeling of uneasiness, of sadness almost, that resolved itself into one thought when we examined it : we are at war.

At first we were not allowed off the camp at all, but eventually we managed to get out for a bathe at West Wittering. At that time I don't think there was one of us who expected to plunge into the cool blue sea again, and then lie on the warm sand in the sun, or to skim over the waters of Chichester Harbour in a yacht, or to drive down to the " Old Ship " at Bosham in the evening and, with the cool air blowing through his hair, drink pints of beer or cider beneath the oak rafters. No one expected to go round the golf course at Goodwood again, or to see the races, or to walk over the Downs. Two nights before our departure for France the Squadron was allowed to go to the " Dolphin and Anchor " at " Chi.," and everyone concealed his depression, and laughed and talked and " knocked it back." But we were all thinking the same thing.

On Friday, September 8th, I was getting a few

minutes' sleep in my room when my father walked in at about 9.30 a.m. I was very glad to see him, and we sat and talked of nothing in particular. At 10.30 my batman dashed in to say : " No. 1 Squadron called to readiness, sir! "—and I hurried down to the aerodrome with the others. We were soon grouped by our machines on the far side of it, and as they were started up one by one, " Leak " took a photograph of us. We tore the squadron badges off our overalls (by order), and I gave mine to a fitter to give to my father, who was leaning over the fence watching us. We jumped into our cockpits, and as I taxied out I waved him good-bye.

We took off in sections, joining up, after a brief individual " beat-up," into Flights in sections-astern, and then line-astern. Down to Beachy Head, then, and with a last look at the cliffs of England we turned out across the water. As we did so, over the R/T from Tangmere came a farewell from our old friends and rivals : " Good Luck from 43 Squadron." There was not a cloud in the sky, scarcely a breath of wind on the sea, and the heat in the cockpits was almost unbearable, for we wore all our gear—full uniform, overalls, web-equipment, respirator slung, and " Mae West." Only the almost complete absence of shipping in the Channel brought home to us that there was a war on somewhere. In about thirty minutes Dieppe appeared through the heat haze, and we turned down the coast toward Le Havre.

Our aerodrome at Le Havre lay N.W. of the town, on the edge of the cliffs, which were some 400 feet high. It was large and new, with an unfinished hangar on one side, and among some trees on another was a long low building that turned out to be a convent which had been commandeered for us to live in. The Squadron closed in, broke up into Flights, then sections, and after saluting the town, came in to land individually. Taxying in, we found our troops ready to welcome us : No. 1 Squadron had arrived in France, the first of the British Fighter Units to do so.

The evening was spent in the town—the "Guillaume Tell," the "Normandie" and "La Lune" following each other in rapid succession. "La Lune," I may add, was one of those places, but its main attraction for us was that its drinking amenities were untrammelled by any such trifling consideration as time. The town seemed to be full of Americans who were endeavouring to escape from the war-zone to the States, and a very cheery lot they were. They were full of admiration for the little bit of formation-flying they had seen us doing when we arrived. They were full of other things too, and "a good time was had by all."

The next day saw us on our feet once more, sober and very, very sorry. However, our Squadron Leader ("the Bull") lost no time in ridding us of our hangovers, and the next three hours were spent in digging a trench in the orchard for our own use in the event of a raid. The sun beat down on our sweating bodies and reeling heads unmercifully, and the alcohol literally poured out of us. At eleven we stopped work—as a matter of fact, there was not one of us who was capable of lifting pick or shovel even once more. Buckets of cold water from the pump pulled us round a little—and then over to our planes for a Squadron Formation.

Soon we were in the cockpits, most of us in shirt-sleeves, and engine after engine burst into life and was run up by its pilot. Then over the R/T, from the Squadron Leader, came : "Come on, we're off, we're off," and he taxied past us, followed by "Hilly" and Leslie, who formed his section. Then came Johnny, "Pussy" and Sgt. S——, who formed the Red Section of "A" Flight, followed by "Leak," myself, and "Stratters," who formed the Yellow. Next came "B" Flight—Prosser, "Boy," and Sgt. B—— (Blue), and Billy, Sgt. C——, and Sgt. A—— (Green).

The fifteen machines moved forward with a deep roar, slowly at first, then gathering speed. Tails were up, and controls getting more "feel." Bump—

bump—bump. Almost off. A bit menacing, this take-off. We fly. No . . . down we come again. Bump. . . . Blast! Must have been a down-draught there. Hold it. We're off now, anyway—straight over the cliff edge and 400 feet above the sea. Prosser shut his eyes in mock terror, and I must say it was an odd feeling. Wheels up. Keep in. Stick between knees. Come on you bloody wheels. Dropping behind a bit. Come on, open your throttle. More. Wide. Ah, there are the two little red lights. Now for God's sake get in closer. Bull's giving it too much throttle, blast him. Anyway, we're there now. There. That's nice.

"Sections astern—Sections astern—Go!" Back a bit. A little left, and underneath. There we are. Don't waffle, Pussy, or I'll be eating up your tail. Up we go. God, it's hot! However, I'm sure it looks nice. Hope so, anyway.

Out we go, over the sea. Going south now, I think. Yes, there's the other side of the Seine. "Turning right—turning right a bit." Round and out to sea again. Keep below—that's right. God, the sun's bloody bright. I can hardly see Prosser's wing when he's above me in a turn. Don't hit him. Look at his tail-plane. "Coming out—coming out." Ah, that's better. "For No. 5 attack—deploy—Go!" "Sections line astern—Go!" "No. 5 attack—Go!"

Open out a bit. There goes Johnny. Now Pussy. There's S——. Prosser's turn now. Me next. *Down* we go. Watch "B" Flight. Pull up now. Fire. Break away. Right over and down to the right. Rejoin. Where the hell's Prosser? Can't see a damn thing. Ah, there he is, up there. Full throttle. Up, up—cut the corner off. Here we come, behind him. Throttle back, or you'll pass him. There we are again.

He's shaking his wings. Form Vic. "Re-form—re-form." "Come on, 'B' Flight, re-form!" "Turning right now." Towards Havre, I suppose. Yes, there it is, right ahead. "Sections echelon star-

4

board—Go." Right. Up. Left. Keep in. There, that's nice, very nice. Now, of your best, please, 1 Squadron. Hope we don't overshoot. No, here we go. " Peel off—peel off—Go ! " There goes the Bull's section. Now Johnny's. Don't watch them— watch Prosser. Here we go now. Down, down, and left a bit. Keep right in—tucked right in. Stratters is O.K. the other side. Right a bit. The controls are getting bloody stiff—must be doing a good 380. Flattening out now. Don't waffle. There's the port. Buildings flashing by underneath. We're nice and low, anyway. Keep in. *Hold it*. Strong arms and strong nerves. Pulling up now—up—over the rise— over the aerodrome now. Down we go again—just to make the Frogs lie down. Up over the trees—just ! Round, and back again. Good fun this—must look all right, too. Bet they're enjoying it. I am ! Here we go again at the trees. Pull up—back she comes. Prosser's waving his hand—break away. There goes Stratters' belly—away we go, nicely timed, in a Prince of Wales.

What now ? God, I feel ill. Let's give the old girl a last shake-up. How about an upward roll ? Yes, good idea—but watch the others. God, the air's full of flying bodies. Let's climb. Now down over there. Want a bit of speed for this. 300—350—360. That's enough. Adjust the wheel. Now back. Gently. Up—up—a bit harder now. Horizon gone —look outwards along the wing. Wait till she's vertical—now, look up. Stick central, now over. Round she goes. Stop. Back with the stick. Look back. There's the horizon again—stick forward— now over, and out we roll. Not bad. God ! Don't look now, but I think I'm going to be sick.

/Let's land, anyway. Slow down. 160. That's O.K.—wheels down. Now flaps. Turn in now. Keep it at 90—tail-wheel right back. Over the boundary. Hold off a bit. Down, down—right back now, bump, rumble, rumble, rumble—there we are. No brakes—plenty of room. Wee bit heavy, that one.

B*

Not quite right. Oh well, no matter. Taxi in—run her out, switch off, brakes off.

*   *   *   *   *

After lunch, trench-digging again. We were determined to finish the rotten thing before tea, in spite of blistered hands and sore backs. At four we were all half-dead, but the trench was practically ready. We were just heaving the last arm-straining shovelfuls out when the Bull came along.

" O.K., boys, you won't need *that* to-night. We're leaving for Cherbourg in half an hour."

" Well I'm ——! " said someone; and that just about summed up the feelings of all of us.

*   *   *   *   *

On our return from Cherbourg there was little doing for a few days. The time was mostly spent in playing with a rugger ball, going down the 400-foot cliff to bathe, sleeping, writing letters, or reading the few papers that came from England every day by air. Our evenings usually started in the " Guillaume Tell " at about six, where we sat over our pernods or vermouths watching the life of the boulevards, and ended in the " Normandie," or elsewhere. I think we all felt that our first taste of service in France would probably be our last of civilization and peace for a long time, and wanted to make the best of it. Personally, I shall always remember with gratitude Le Havre, with its fine port, its magnificent view from the hill across to Deauville, its wide boulevards, cafés, shops and restaurants—and its church of St. Michel, where the old Curé preached such a moving sermon to the Mothers of France, and afterwards heard my Confession and gave me so much strength and courage.

We left Le Havre on September 29th. I was flying a reserve machine without parachute or sights, and so had to proceed independently though within sight of the formation. I took off first and climbed to 8,000 feet in brilliant sunshine and slight haze. There

6

I circled slowly, and with difficulty watched the Squadron leave the aerodrome and creep out over the sea. I could hear them chattering away, but completely lost sight of them over the land. However, coming down to 5,000 feet I picked them out beating up Le Havre. They looked like a tiny slug crawling over the town, although there were five sections in sections-astern : nice and close. After they had gone I came down in a series of horrid twists and inversions, and having said good-bye to the town in general, and to one or two people in particular, in a certain way, I headed in the direction they had taken.

And so, I thought, to war. . . . That day our A.O.C. had inspected us and told us in guarded terms what we were in for. He had summarised the situation thus : the Fighter Squadrons were responsible for the air protection of the British Field Force —that was, all units, army and air alike—in France. It was considered that, sooner or later, Germany would launch a terrific offensive on the Western Front, and would violate Belgium and/or Luxembourgian neutrality to achieve her aim of breaking through. In Poland, German attacks had been preceded by a thorough aerial bombardment of all military concentrations, and particularly of aerodromes. Our job was to stop them, or at any rate to make things so hot for them that they would have to relent. The French would help us of course—but even then it was obvious that we would have to bear the brunt of the attack. Good. We believed our equipment better than the Germans'. Our personnel could not have been improved, and our morale was of the highest. Fighting would be hard and continual, and, speaking from a personal point of view, many of us would probably be killed. Four squadrons against the German Luftwaffe! It looked absurd. But at least we were not afraid to fight, or if necessary to die, and were confident that we should give a good account of ourselves.

* * * * *

The British Air Forces in France, or B.A.F.F., were split into two parts : the Air Component, with G.H.Q. at Amiens, which operated over Northern France from the coast as far down as Le Havre to the Belgian Frontier some way S.E. of Lille, co-operating with the British Army ; and the Advanced Air Striking Force, with G.H.Q. at Reims, which operated variously along the Belgian and Luxembourg Frontiers and along and across the German Frontier between Luxembourg and Lauterbourg in co-operation with the French Army and Air Force. The Air Component was commanded by an Air Vice-Marshal, and originally comprised, as far as I know, four Hurricane Squadrons, two Gladiator Squadrons, one or two Blenheim Squadrons, and one or two Lysander Squadrons. The Fighter Squadrons had to do quite a lot of work over the sea, mostly protecting convoys. The Advanced Air Striking Force, or A.A.S.F., was commanded by another Air Vice-Marshal, and was composed of Bomber Squadrons dotted around H.Q.—Battles and Blenheims.

After leaving Le Havre, 1 and 73 Squadrons (two of the four Hurricane Squadrons in the Air Component) were kicking their heels at Norrent, not far from St. Omer. However, when some of our Battles were shot up by Messerschmitts over the Franco-German frontier, our C.O. thought it would be a good thing if we could go and lend the bombers a hand. Accordingly, 1 and 73 Squadrons moved down, we to Vassincourt aerodrome, near Bar-le-Duc, and 73 to Etain-Rouvres aerodrome, near Verdun. Together we formed 67 Wing.

Our first few months at Vassincourt were uneventful. The aerodrome was on a hill, and surrounded by woods. At the foot of the hill passed a canal and a railway-line, and on the other side of these lay the little village of Neuville, where we were billeted. There were many old houses there, and also many scars of the last war. The Germans had been there both in 1870 and 1914, and the inhabitants bore them no great love. My own billet was in a very old farm-house, half-timbered, gabled and rambling. My host, of whom more later, worked on the railway as a signalman.

I cannot remember the exact date of our first victory, but I believe it was November 1st. It was a beautiful sunny day, with no low clouds but quite a lot of Cirrus and Cirrostratus, and a bit of Alto-cumulus. I was on the aerodrome by my machine when we heard the noise of unfamiliar aircraft engines. After a lot of neck-craning and squinting we saw it—a Dornier 17 immediately above the aerodrome at about 20,000 feet, travelling west and just visible in the thinner clouds. Like all German aircraft of the Luftwaffe it was painted light-blue underneath, and was difficult to see. The French A.A. opened up but were nowhere near it.

This was the first Hun we'd seen, and we were pretty excited. Sgt. S—— and I took off in pursuit, but of course had to watch our take-off and lost him. At 3,000 feet we saw him again, but lost him soon after. Up and up we clambered, turning gently from side to side and straining our eyes to find him. We never saw him again, and at 25,000 feet, with our sights alight and gun-buttons on "Fire," we cursed like hell and came down after some fifteen minutes' search.

After lunch we went up to the aerodrome again. Not long afterwards a Hurricane dived across the field rocking its wings, turned, came back, and repeated the performance in an obviously excited manner. It turned out to be "Boy," who had come to the Squadron in June. He had apparently just finished refuelling after a patrol over the aerodrome when the same Dornier went over. He took off immediately, without waiting for orders, pulled the "plug" (boost-override), lost the Hun, clambered up to about 18,000 feet—and found him. He did an ordinary straight astern attack, and fired one longish burst with his sights starting above the Dornier and moving slowly round the fuselage. The Hun caught fire immediately, went into a vertical spiral, and eventually made a large hole in the French countryside. It exploded on striking the ground, and there were no survivors. The remains of a gun from the machine, together with a bullet-pierced oxygen-bottle, from now on adorned our Mess as trophies of the first British Fighter victory of the war—which was also the first Fighter engagement—in France.

The remains of the Nazi airmen—five hands—were given a funeral with military honours, at which the Squadron was represented. Naturally we were all glad of our first trial, but we were sorry for the poor young devils we had downed. " Boy " got rather drunk that night, and said to me, " You know I'm damn' sorry I went and looked at the thing; and what gets me down is the thought that *I* did it. . . ."

*   *   *   *   *

For some three weeks after this incident life was quiet—principally because of bad weather. The rains came, and the countryside was flooded. However, one day (November 23rd) the sun set in a blaze of red as the clouds broke, and the following morning was sunny and clear. It was my ill-fortune to be on duty in the Operations Room that day, and there was plenty to think about, too. Soon the map was covered with " plots," and we sent patrols off " round the houses " to see what they could do about it. They did quite a lot : we bagged two Dorniers 17, with a " share " in a Heinkel 111 (a third went to the French A.A., a third to 73 Squadron, and a third to us); 73 also got three Dorniers, *plus* the above-mentioned " share." Most of the enemy aircraft crashed in flames, but there were some survivors, mostly wounded, who escaped by parachute.

Of our two Dorniers, one was intercepted by the Bull and Hilly near Metz. They attacked alternately and continually from astern until the Hun went into a steep spiral and crashed in flames near the lines. So far as I know there were no survivors. I remember talking to the C.O. over the R/T and hearing him sing out : " It's all right, we've got another one for the Squadron near ——." " Near where ? " I asked, " Say again," and he repeated "Homburg, as in hat ! "

The Heinkel 111 was also brought down near Metz, and was intercepted by Blue Section. It was on fire, and losing height rapidly, when a bunch of French Moranes came rushing in, all so eager to have a bang that one of them knocked most of Sgt. C——'s tail off. He put up a very good show by getting the machine back to the aerodrome, though he had to land at 120 m.p.h. to keep control, overshooting and turning over. I saw him just after this little effort, and though he was laughing, he was trembling like a leaf and could hardly talk coherently. I saw his aircraft, too : one elevator and half the rudder were completely gone. I believe the Frenchman jumped for it. Anyway, the Heinkel came down all right—but to our disgust we were only officially credited with one-third of it, as I have just mentioned.

A section from 1 Squadron, led by Pussy, attacked the other Dornier about 20 miles north of the aerodrome. Pussy led the attack from dead astern. By the time he had used all his ammunition the rear-gunner and navigator had escaped by parachute, one engine was on fire, and the Dornier was losing height and appeared to be more or less out of control. Pussy then flew alongside the German to make sure the pilot was dead. He saw him slumped in his seat, his head lolling to one side. Suddenly, however, the Dornier throttled back, swerved on to Pussy's tail, and put exactly 34 bullets through his aircraft. Hearing them rip through Pussy ducked—thereby saving his life, for a bullet penetrated the locker behind his head, smashing the windscreen—and pushed his stick forward. Clouds of white smoke (which proved to be glycol) were pouring from his engine, which was stopped, and Pussy undid his straps and prepared to bale out. The " smoke " stopped, however—presumably the glycol was all gone—and so he did his straps up again and forced-landed safely with his undercarriage retracted. Meanwhile, Killy and S——, Nos. 2 and 3 of Pussy's section, attacked, and with both engines on fire the German forced-landed more or less safely. Killy and S—— circled round and saw him wave as they passed low overhead. They then returned and landed. Pussy was sent for by car.

The Dornier was found to have at least 500 bullet-holes in it—not enough, considering that three Hurricanes had had a go at it. Apparently the pilot had had to leave his seat to lock the gun with which he had shot Pussy down. We all felt that this German had put up a damned good show, and as a tribute to the spirit that all pilots admire, we determined to have him to dine with us as our guest. The French authorities were very reluctant to part with him, but eventually he was allowed to come with Billy, whom we had sent to fetch him.

He turned out to be a non-commissioned officer of some experience. Suspicious at first, he melted as he realized our goodwill, and we gave him the best dinner we could muster under the circumstances. Everything went very well except for one awkward incident. Mistaking Hilly's laughter at a joke for amusement at his plight, the German got very serious, and then suddenly broke down. We all understood that he must be now a little overwrought after his ordeal in the air and his capture, so were not as surprised as we might otherwise have been. On being taken outside he quickly pulled himself together—adding to his apologies the explanation that he was fed up with the war. He left us at 1 a.m.—all of us being by then pretty merry—the richer by several articles of warm clothing, and vainly requesting that he should be sent to England in between assurances that we would be treated with equal kindness should we be taken prisoner by his countrymen.

*　　*　　*　　*　　*

The following six weeks were deadly dull again. Weather generally was bad, and enemy activity slight. Eventually, on December 19th, the first Leave Party from the A.A.S.F. left, and as I was getting married, I was one of the lucky ones.

Shortly after my return (i.e., in January), I was sent up to " Wing." Wing, of course, was 67 Wing H.Q., and was situated in a pleasant house in a small village some two miles from our own, called Bussy-la-Côte. As its name suggested, it stood on a hill, overlooking a small valley through which ran a stream, the railway and a canal, and almost facing the far end of the aerodrome. My duties (Operations) were not arduous, and I shared them with P—— (the Squadron Leader Ops.) and a pilot from 73 Squadron. I was glad enough to be there, for the weather was bitterly cold. There was no flying, and I could live in a warm house with good food and a comfortable sitting-room.

My ample time off-duty was spent in reading, writing letters, writing my diary, and playing soccer with the Padre, Henry (the Army Signals officer) and the troops (once we enticed a bunch of French *poilus* of Le Génie (engineers) away from their sergeant, much to his annoyance). Sometimes I would go for a walk by myself along the valley, where I one day found an old deserted house and took some photographs of the beautiful ice-formations round a water-fall in the grounds. On another occasion, some of us tried our hands at navigating a rude flat-bottomed boat up the stream. Shooting with service rifles from the terrace of the house high above the stream at empty petrol cans down on the other side was another of our pastimes—but one not too popular with the French cowherds. Spy-baiting was yet another game. F—— (the R.A.F. Signals officer) had spy-mania, and was convinced that there was a wireless-jamming machine in the village that interfered with our R/T. Certainly there was jamming when we were trying to effect interceptions on enemy machines, but it probably came from Germany. However, F—— was sure it

13

didn't, and strongly suspected a certain house kept by a woman who had some very fierce dogs in her yard. He used to creep about the village in the dead of night, climbing her wall and generally poking round. He declared that her dogs were deliberately kept hungry to keep them fierce, and was certain that she was hiding something. Accordingly he set himself to visit the dogs every night to feed them and gradually tame them, until eventually they didn't try to harm him or even bark. However, I don't think his sleuthing ever bore fruit.

Then there was the Blind Professor. The Blind Professor had (so it seemed) been a professor at the University of Nancy, but had been evacuated to Bussy (no one quite knew why). He had a little room on the far side of the garage which adjoined our house, where he used to sit typing in Braille most of the day and far into the night. A curious thing about him was that whenever a car passed he used to have no trouble in running outside, which necessitated negotiating two doorways and several steps, and looking up and down the road to see who it was. Another curious thing was that one day something went wrong with the telephones, and the operational messages from Panther (H.Q. at Reims) to our Ops. Room came through to the telephone in the garage—which the Professor was not slow in answering himself. I am quite certain the man was a spy, but no one seemed to bother much about him. Apparently the French police, who were supposed to deal with such matters, had him on their list of " suspects," and probably were watching him after a fashion.

All this does not seem so unlikely in the light of after events which revealed the German spy-system in France. At Châlons-sur-Marne, for instance, they later found a telephone-line in a room beneath the station-master's office communicating direct with Germany. Certainly some fishy things went on round Wing and our village, as when, for instance, a man, ostensibly a " tourist " from Bar-le-Duc, walked around Neuville photographing the transport. The troops thought little of it, and by the time one of our officers heard about it he'd driven away. Again, P—— once came into the Mess after dark looking rather white, and said that someone had fired at him as he went up the steps; we never found the culprit, of course. On another occasion I took a new Armament officer (who'd come to us in error) from Wing down to the Squadron; we were driven down a short-cut back road, and I had intended leaving the officer and hurrying back to supper. However, after a few drinks in the Mess with the boys I decided to stay, and sent the driver back. When I was eventually collected and returned to Wing, I learnt that on the way up someone had taken a pot at the car from a wood on the edge of the road, the bullet smashing the windscreen just in front of where I had been sitting and lodging in the door. The driver ran off the road and lay doggo for a few minutes, gun in hand; but no one came, so he drove on as fast as he could. The French police took over, but found nothing—except that the bullet seemed to be from a British .45 revolver, which only the Signalmen had. The short-cut was subsequently forbidden after dark, but I took it several times on foot to see what I should see.

All one's fears and suspicions seem a trifle absurd at a distance, but there undoubtedly were queer happenings in France. While at Wing I always carried a gun at night, and in my hand, fully cocked, and always walked in the middle of the road with my ears and eyes very much open and an occasional glance behind. In bed in my billet (which was at the far end of the village), I kept my gun under the mattress beside me.

Yes, Bussy was a funny little village, with its air of mystery, of evil almost. But I prefer to remember it as I sometimes saw it from the valley, with the evening sun glinting on its snow-covered roofs and gilding the square Italian tower of its deserted little church.

* * * * *

On my return to the Squadron the weather mercifully improved, and I was not sorry to fly again. Not having been able to do much reconnaissance during the bad weather, the Huns now made up for lost time, and there was the promise of action. 73 Squadron, because of its position, had more chance of this than we had, for the Huns' regular route seemed to be across the Moselle at the corner of Luxembourg; they came over in large formations, splitting up near the frontier and going on their various missions. 73 often saw them pass over their aerodrome, and brought one down now and then.

In 1 Squadron we were getting pretty impatient for action by this time, and cursed our luck at not having yet seen any fighters (73 had had more luck in this respect than we had). It still remained the Squadron's policy, nevertheless, to be cautious and bide our time, and there's no doubt it was the right one. We seldom crossed the frontier, and when we did we went over as high as possible and did a " sweep " round in a semi-circle and back again to draw the German fighters out. After all, one would look silly if one fell prisoner. If we saw something, of course, we'd cross and attack it if it was within reasonable distance; but the Squadron's watchword was " Caution." No fooling, no dare-devil ace stuff, no individual seeking the limelight. This time was a training one, and very useful experience. Our turn would come with the German push, and when it did, we would be ready as a well-trained team, all having seen a little action, and all well-versed in the art of team-fighting.

Soon after my return from Wing came our fifth victory. Hilly, Sgt. S——, and " Mitch " (a new pilot) were on patrol near Nancy when they sighted a Do.17. Unfortunately, just about the same time Hilly's prop (a wooden one) flew into small pieces for no particular reason, and he forced-landed on Nancy aerodrome with his wheels up. S—— and Mitch attacked the Dornier alternately from astern. S—— was still attacking when he heard Mitch call, " I'm hit

16

5   " B " FLIGHT AT READINESS
(*Left to Right :* Peter M——, Peter B——, Leslie, Prosser, Lorry and Sammy)

6   MEMBERS OF 73 SQUADRON
(*Left to Right :* A Sergeant Pilot, " Ginger " P——, " Fanny " O——, and " Cobber "

7   BATTLES RETURNING FROM A RAID

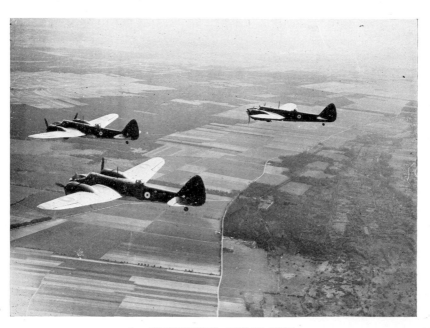

8   BLENHEIMS GOING OUT

in the engine and must go down "; so he left the
Dornier, which was by now on fire and low down (it
subsequently crashed), and returned to find a field for
Mitch, who couldn't see much for smoke. He picked
a field, watched Mitch approach, and then lost him
completely. We learned later that he had spun in on
the edge of the field, or else hit a tree (onlookers' state-
ments varied), and was killed. This was our first
casualty. Mitch was a New Zealander, and was
shaping well. He was a big, cheerful youngster, and
a Catholic. He had lent me his pen the night before
his death (March 2nd, 1940), and I am using it now.

The following day, the 3rd, came our sixth victory.
Hilly and Sgt. S—— were again concerned. Between
Nancy and Metz they sighted a He.111K at about
24,000 feet. Hilly climbed beside and at some distance
from it, but S—— tried to attack from underneath and
spun. Hilly eventually got above it and attacked by
diving from astern. Soon S—— was back again, and
between them they set fire to both engines and saw the
Heinkel forced-land between the French and German
lines. Two men got out of it and ran for the German
side, which they apparently reached.

Here came a pause. The weather was bad, and the
cold intense. Snow and ice were everywhere, and it
was impossible to keep warm, indoors or out. In the
Mess we used to keep a large kettle continually simmer-
ing on the stove, from which we would make ourselves
hot grogs, bovril, and so on. The winter everywhere
was quite exceptionally cold, and, of course, we were
no worse off than many others. Still, patrolling at
25,000 feet, or sitting in a tent on the aerodrome from
dawn till dusk, was not at all funny.

One incident that occurred at about this time is
perhaps worth recording. I took off alone one sunny
morning to test my guns at 25,000 feet, and as always
on those occasions when we had the time, headed
towards the lines to fire them into Germany. On the
way I had to climb through a couple of layers of cloud,
but it was clear again over Nancy, and I could see the

Moselle curving away towards Metz. I continued to climb, keeping a sharp look-out, but it was difficult to realize that there was a war on. I crossed the lines at 27,000 feet; there was a layer of cloud between the frontier and Nancy at 10,000 feet, and another starting some distance the other side of the frontier and stretching away, flat and soft and peaceful, into the heart of Germany. The country below me for some distance on either side of the frontier showed no signs of life : no smoke from the chimneys, no traffic on the roads, no boats on the canals. Towns and hills, winding rivers and dark-green, rolling forests were below me; flat white cloud-layers, blue sky and brilliant sun above; and far away to the S.E. (some 300 miles to be exact), believe it or not, were the white snow-peaks of the Alps.

All this made a very lovely picture, filling me with that curious sensation of aloofness and remoteness that only the pilot knows. It often requires a strong physical effort to wrench oneself away from this dreaming at high altitude, and the mind tends to wander in a curious way. Scientists say it is lack of oxygen, but I think there are other causes too. At any rate, I was hunting on this occasion, and could not allow my mind to wander; so I concentrated my thoughts once more on the watchers on the ground, on the anti-aircraft guns, and on the stalking Messerschmitts. I kept turning my aeroplane from one side to the other, sometimes doing a complete circle, and twisted my head and eyes round continuously, searching every corner of the sky and paying special attention to my tail and to that bright but treacherous sun. Now and again I fired my guns, and was comforted to feel the shudder of the aircraft and to see the converging streams of incendiaries leaping out ahead.

After floating round Saarbrücken and about 40 miles into Germany for about 30 minutes, I turned for home. The clouds were getting thicker below me, and I decided to come down over Verdun, as I thought. I dived down through several layers of thick cloud, and eventually found myself above a final layer at 1,000 feet. I found a hole and went down through it gently, to find it very dark and visibility bad. I then saw a fair-sized town and flew over it without recognising it. Shortly afterwards I found another town with an aerodrome. On the edge of the aerodrome was a hospital prominently marked with the Red Cross, and in the centre of the field a large circle with ESCH written in white in the middle. I couldn't find Esch on my map, and I didn't much like the sound of it, so flew away. By this time petrol was low, so I flew south for a few minutes and then began looking for an aerodrome. I eventually found a town which had one, but it looked small, and so I tried to get home. I thought the town was St. Menehould, but after flying down a valley for some ten minutes, past factories and railway lines, I made up my mind to be lost and returned to the aerodrome. I was by this time so short of petrol that I made a forced-landing approach. The aerodrome was very boggy and I all but turned over. I taxied in to find I was at Thionville. Esch, I learned, was in Luxembourg, and the town I flew over was the capital, so I came near to emulating " Dicky," of 73 Squadron, who was the "Prisoner of Luxembourg" for some weeks. His escape, incidentally, was amusing. Every day he was exercised in an open space by an officer. He induced this officer to buy him a map of Luxembourg, as he said he was interested in its history and topography. Christmas Day dawned foggy, and so Dicky thought up a plan. At exercise he showed such amazing vigour in walking back and forth that his officer-guard eventually got fed up with it and stopped. Dicky, however, asked to be allowed to walk on, and was given permission to do so up and down in front of the exhausted officer. He went on and on, back and forth, each time moving a little farther away before turning. Finally he just walked straight off, was swallowed in the fog, ran like hell, and after some days managed to reach France again.

He was nearly shot as a spy, of course, but was eventually returned to his Squadron.

*　　*　　*　　*　　*

|Soon after this came our seventh victory. I always thought seven was my lucky number, and this time it was. I was on patrol near Metz at about 9 a.m., with Pussy leading and Peter M—— (who joined us in France) No. 3 behind me. At 20,000 feet I sighted A.A. fire N.E. of us at 15,000 feet, and flew towards it, Pussy seeing the aircraft that was being fired at. I never saw it, and, anyway, it disappeared shortly afterwards. We were searching for it, being by now at about 25,000 feet, when I saw two Messerschmitt 109's above us to our left, travelling in the opposite direction. While climbing to attack these we heard Peter call : "Look out behind!" Three others were now attacking us from the rear. Peter was being fired at, and blacked out getting out of the way, coming to at 10,000 feet. Pussy dived steeply to the left, turning, and then spinning. Thinking he had mistaken me for a Hun I called, "It's only me." However, he'd gone by then, so I continued to climb in a left-hand turn, but watching my tail.

I saw an aircraft coming up behind, but wasn't sure whether he was a Hurricane or Messerschmitt, so waited for him to open fire. He did, at longish range, and I twisted down underneath his nose and flattened out violently. As I did so, either he or one of the two above came down on my port quarter and shot by just above my cockpit. He was so close that I heard his engine and felt the air-wave. He pulled up in front of me, stall-turned to the left, and dived down with me on his tail. He was much faster and I couldn't get within range, so held fire. He went down about 10,000 feet, pulled up violently at 50 degrees or so, then throttled back at the top of a straight climb, and I caught him up.

Waiting till he was sitting pretty, I let him have it. Unfortunately my gun-button was sticking in and I wasted a lot of ammunition; still, he soon started to pour out smoke. I think the pilot must have been hit, for he took no violent evasive action, merely falling slowly to the right in a steep spiral. I was by this time a bit excited, and unfortunately dived down on top of him and used my remaining ammunition. I then pulled out and saw another Messerschmitt about 2,000 feet above. He came towards me, but knowing his speed to be superior I didn't beat it but turned towards him, partly to stop him getting on my tail and partly to bluff him. Either he had no ammunition left (unlikely, for they carried 1,000 rounds for each gun to our 300), or he'd seen his companion go down and wasn't feeling so brave. Anyway, he made off, and so did I—at ground level until I reached Nancy. Unfortunately my 109 must have fallen near Merzig in Germany, and was therefore not confirmed from the ground. Pussy and Peter were miles away at the time and saw nothing.

The same day, a little later, Johnny eclipsed my getting the Squadron's first enemy fighter by getting the first Messerschmitt 110 in France. He, Stratters and Sgt. C—— sighted nine of them, the first to appear in France, north of Metz. They climbed to attack, Johnny getting behind one and sticking to it through some violent manœuvres—vertical stall-turns and so on. He followed it through cloud, saw it catch fire, and ran out of ammunition. It was later found in small pieces, the pilot having escaped by parachute. C—— had a bang at two, but was uncertain of the result. Stratters either attacked another or Johnny's—probably the latter. Anyway, the three of them were given the reward the Air Marshal commanding B.A.F.F. had promised a few days before to the first pilot to get a Me.110 on the Western Front: dinner with him in Paris. The A.O.C.-in-C.'s personal aircraft (a Percival Q.6) collected the boys, and they dined at Maxim's—quite rightly, I think.

That evening, as was our custom, the victors

partook of the special bottle of rum reserved for those occasions, drank the toast, " To past members of 1 Squadron," and filled in and signed our Victory Card. Naturally a party was not long in materialising, and we " passed out " *via* the Sergeants' Mess (which, incidentally, had been got up to look as much like an English country pub as possible, with a bar, beer-barrel seats and tables, and a large open hearth). I remember going over to the village church opposite our Mess to say a prayer for the German I had killed before I got too boozy. The door was locked, so I knelt on the steps and prayed for him and his family and those who loved him, and for Germany.

*　　*　　*　　*　　*

On March 31st Prosser, Leslie and Boy ran into nine Me.110's near Metz. They climbed to attack, and the 110's dived down on them, one opening fire head-on at Prosser, who replied. He got a shell in his oil-tank (port wing), but continued to fight. After the engagement each pilot claimed a 110.

On April 1st, Leslie, Lew, Lorry, Pussy and Killy went on patrol near Nancy. I got off late through starting difficulty, and couldn't find them. They sighted a Do.17, gave chase, and were attacked by Me.109's (probably five). Pussy got a shell in his front tank before he knew where he was, inverted his machine and baled out, the machine crashing in flames. He himself landed 300 yards inside the French lines and had quite a party with the local infantry regiment (the famous " Diables Rouges "). The other boys had a short fight, Killy getting a 109 (confirmed from the ground, but falling in Germany), and Leslie claiming another.

Meanwhile, I was messing about at 25,000 feet north of Metz, where I thought the boys would be. All I saw were half a dozen Moranes and a lot of cloud beneath me. Eventually I went down through broken cloud, thinking I was near Thionville. At

9,000 feet I got properly peppered by quick-firers and took violent evasive action. I was actually over Trier, some 30 miles inside Germany, so flew down the Moselle at no mean speed. I landed at Metz for petrol, but broke a tail-wheel taxying in, and so got stuck for a couple of days.

I landed simultaneously with the Moranes I had seen. They had had a combat and were greatly excited, the victors naturally being especially jubilant. The Commandant of the Morane Squadron sent a pilot for my new tail-wheel, and those excellent French mechanics had it on by evening. However, the weather came down, so I stayed. I spent my time wandering round the town, looking at the shops, the gardens and the cathedral—and at the women, who are famous for their beauty. Later that evening there was a big farewell dinner at the Réunion (Officers' Club) to the General commanding the district. I managed to borrow a shirt and some shoes to exchange for my roll-neck jersey and flying-boots, but my old uniform looked a bit battered. However, no one seemed to mind. After dinner we all sang, and as the rifles and sabres on the walls of the great hall rattled to the roar of " Saint-Cyr, Garde à Vous," " La Madelon," " Les Artilleurs de Metz," the " Marche Lorraine," and many other famous French marches, one seemed transported into the days when Metz was a garrison town whose cobbled streets rang to the clatter of cavalry and horse artillery, and whose cafés and restaurants were crowded with brilliant uniforms. " Roll out the Barrel," which was sung by the British, was encored several times by the French, and proved a great favourite. It's a good marching song, but it lacked that quality of elation possessed by the French marches; and it dispelled all dreams of an army of long ago, bringing us back to the tanks and drab uniforms of modern warfare.

*　　*　　*　　*　　*

23

One morning Pussy, Killy and I did our usual patrol round Metz and Nancy, and eastwards from there, but as usual were disappointed. On the way back, as was our habit, we did a spot of dog-fighting among ourselves, and beat up Velaine (a French fighter station between Toul and Nancy) in a mild sort of way. I followed Pussy down close behind from 15,000 to about 1,000 feet. We were doing a hell of a speed, and Pussy was giving out black smoke (because he was at full throttle), so I broke away and followed him up in a couple of climbing rolls. We left the forest behind us and slid lazily back to Bar-le-Duc, basking in the warm sunshine, to park down on the aerodrome once more at Vassincourt, taxi over to the tankers and refuel.

Having switched off, I jumped down to chat with Killy, who was already there. We glanced at the sunny sky now and then from force of habit. There were a lot of condensation-trails about, but mostly at some distance, visibility being perfect. Suddenly we heard the familiar sound of Hun engines, and we both stopped talking and looked up, shielding our eyes with our hands.

"There she is—a Hun all right!" I said, and pointed to the small but clearly visible outline, duck-egg blue underside glinting against the deeper blue of the sky. "Twenty thousand, I'd say—and slap over the aerodrome! *He'll* get some nice pictures . . ." But Killy was already dashing to his machine, which was refuelled and running. He took off in a hell of a hurry, while I ran to my own machine, which wasn't quite ready. However, I suspended the refuelling, started up, and watched the Hun and Killy as I did my straps up. I saw the Hun turn south, but Killy for some reason turned south-east. I took off and climbed south-west, thinking I might cut the Hun off if he resumed his journey westwards, but I lost him in taking off, and though I clambered up to 20,000 feet couldn't see a thing. My oxygen had been showing " o " from the take-off, but there

9   SUNSET AT VASSINCOURT

10   A MORANE 406 BEATS UP VASSINCOURT AERODROME
(A French Curtis Hawk and a Hurricane in the foreground

11 DISPERSAL POINT AT VASSINCOURT

12 KILLY

13 BOY

seemed to be just a little left, and I used it very sparingly and not below 18,000 feet.

I did a wide circle round over Vitry-le-François and Châlons-sur-Marne, climbing and straining my eyes all the while. Not a sign : only a lot of white trails to the N.E. I headed towards them, hoping to find something else, but the aircraft making them was going too fast and was too high. I was beginning to feel very short of oxygen, my height now being 27,000 feet, so I turned just north of St. Menehould towards the aerodrome. Now I was feeling definitely faint : my head was buzzing, my brain and actions were sluggish, and a dark veil was pressing down over my eyes. I remember saying to myself : " Come on, down you go, or you'll pass out "—and I dived at about 50 degrees, forgetting to throttle back, I was so dopey. At 20,000 feet I was awakened from my coma by a very solid " Bang ! " on the tail. I immediately throttled back, thinking, " God ! my bloody tail's coming off," and eased out of the dive very gently, twisting my head round and looking anxiously at the tips of my tail-plane, then at the cowlings on the guns and engine. Everything seemed all right, but I was losing speed unduly slowly. My prop, perhaps . . . I opened the throttle slightly. Yes, that must be it—my prop's bust. The engine turned over very roughly, and suddenly there was another minor jolt, and she ran perfectly smoothly. I throttled right back again, then cautiously opened the throttle, watching my rev. counter. It suddenly swung right round to about 3,000, so I snatched back the throttle and switched off.

This all took far less time than it takes to tell, of course. Well, there I was, 20 miles from the aerodrome with no prop. However, I had 20,000 feet, and could see the aerodrome after looking. It was quite easy really. I arrived over the aerodrome at 9,000 feet. I must say I felt apprehensive on the way down, and had pictures of finishing in the far hedge, or of spinning-in or crashing half a mile away.

But on my last half-circuit, when I knew I was just right and could turn in anywhere I liked if necessary and make it, I actually enjoyed the sensation of gliding silently through the air, with no prop turning over in front and obscuring the view, and no engine shaking the machine. As I climbed out at the end of my run, however, I found to my surprise that my hands were shaking.

Meanwhile, there was no sign of Killy, and as the morning wore on we rather forgot about him. The 'phone rang, and Johnny went off with a section to do a patrol. The rest of us lay basking in the sun, playing the gramophone and reading. Suddenly there was a rush and a roar as a Hurricane dived over us, and we all jumped up excitedly as we saw it rocking its wings and Johnny's "D" on the side. "Good show—I wonder what it was?" we asked each other. Johnny landed and taxied over. We ran out, and he waved his hand with his thumb up. I jumped up on the wing and put my ear close to his face; his brown eyes were bright as he laughed under his oxygen-mask.

"What was it?" I shouted through the slip-stream.

"A 109," came the muffled shout.

At lunch came news of Killy. He was near Paris, and he was as tight as an owl. That evening he was returned to the bosom of the Squadron and told his tale. Apparently he kept the Hun in sight after taking off, lost him, but picked him up again later. The Hun kept turning, and as he drew nearer started climbing. Killy had his "plug" pulled all the time, and eventually managed to get somewhere near the Hun at 27,000 feet, still going west. At last he was near enough to open fire at long range, and the Hun —a Junkers 88—got the wind up and dived. They went right down to ground level, Killy potting away and eventually getting in some close bursts low down. Suddenly Killy's engine, to use his own expression, "blew up" (as the result of return fire), and he forced-landed in great haste with the wheels up and travelling fast.

He wasn't hurt or even burnt, and was soon rescued by the French, who were later responsible for his condition of intoxication. The sun helped, too, Killy said. He was very annoyed at losing his Hun, but spent a pleasant day in the countryside. Later in the evening, however, we learnt that Killy had got his Hun after all : it had crash-landed near Macon, miles from where he had left it. The occupants could not explain why they had flown on the courses they did when attacked, had no idea where they were, and had apparently completely lost their bearings, and to a certain extent their heads, in the fight—which is not at all a difficult thing to do. They had a list of about fifteen towns to be visited on their reconnaissance, and had been to a good many of them when Killy appeared.

On the whole, quite a fruitful and entertaining day. But they weren't *all* like that !

*   *   *   *   *

By this time, of course, the snows had melted, and the trees were once more showing signs of life. The sunshine and showers of April had succeeded the windy dryness of March, and the countryside was beginning to show promise of blossoming into the wealth of fruit and flowers and greenness that the local people predicted for the summer. " Oh oui, le pays est très bon pour les fruits—et les fleurs et les poissons et tout, et tout . . ." the old woman at my billet would tell me. Her husband would come in from his railway work in the evening, and would knock at my door and ask me along to the kitchen to have a drink with him while he ate his supper. " Venez, Monsieur——," he would say, "venez boire un verre," and he would fill my glass with the red vin-du-pays, and we would talk of the war. He would then get very serious. " Ah, oui," he would grunt, shaking his head, " ah, oui." After supper he would say to his wife : "Marie, la bouteille," and she would delve into the big chest and produce the Mirabelle. " Vous prendrez une petite goûte, Monsieur? " he would ask, pouring me out one. I could never refuse, and Madame would simultaneously bring our coffee which she had just ground and made. Sometimes I would grind the coffee. Then Madame used to sit down, and her husband would become confidential.

" Ah, oui," he would say again, this time nodding, " Et je peux vous dire que ce sera très long." He would then roll and light a cigarette, slowly and deliberately. "Oh, pas si long que ça," I would suggest with a shrug, " Trois ans—peut-être quatre." He would look at me for a moment as he puffed his cigarette. Then he would lean forward and tap my knee. " Je ne suis pas de ceux qui disent des choses— et j'en sais beaucoup. Je suis très discret, comprenez-vous, et je ne dis pas tout-ce que je sais. Mais vous êtes militaire, et je peux vous dire que ce sera très long, et très dur. Ah, oui! "

Although we were worlds apart in most things, a great affection sprang up between my hosts and myself. Often the old boy used to drag me out to the little café at the corner, or to the baker's down the road, where he used to take a delight in instructing me in novel, and sometimes very unpleasant, mixtures of alcohol. He was a short, rotund man, thickset and strong in body, with a round, weather-beaten face, black eyes, and a walrus moustache. He was a simple, sincere little man, with a sense of humour. His wife was a big, untidy woman, loud of voice, with a rollicking sense of humour descended straight from Rabelais. She would tell one a joke roaring with laughter and slapping her thigh with delight; but I sometimes used to find her weeping quietly and thinking of her sons; and then she used to say simply, " Oui, j'ai le cafard aujourd'hui. . . ."

Both monsieur and madame were of good old peasant stock of the sort that is the backbone of France: honest, hard-working, simple, kind-hearted, courageous people; content with what they had built up in their farmhouse, self-supporting (if with little to spare), living and dying in their little village, and willing to defend it to the last. But I ought not to finish this sketch of our *ménage* without a mention of Flandin, the big English setter, "worth 700 francs," who fiercely attacked all visitors and bit any stranger who touched him. Much to my hosts' surprise, Flandin and I managed to become great friends, and I could fondle and pet him as much as I liked. He would often come along to see me in my room, and whenever I entered the house used to stand up on his hind-legs, put his paws on my chest, and lick my face—a compliment he had hitherto only paid to his master.

When eventually we left Neuville, I wrote my late host a letter of thanks for his hospitality, enclosing a hundred-franc note for a debt of a few francs for firewood, and requesting him to purchase a bottle of good wine with the change and perhaps drink my health in it. He answered as follows, in the usual violet ink and thin, flowery handwriting :
Monsieur ——,

> I thank you very sincerely for your generosity, of which you are unable to partake; all the same, I would have very much liked to have seen you again, inasmuch as we get on very well together. As you say, "C'est la guerre."
>
> You are an officer of merit, I myself am at my job as you know, with my two sons fighting against a monster that we must destroy at any cost, and I think *that we shall succeed.*
>
> I enclose a letter to you from my son, who is deeply touched. . . .
>
> I and my wife wish you happiness and prosperity for the days to come.
>
> I hope to see you again one of these days if you can manage it.
>
> A brave and honest comrade cordially shakes you by the hand for himself and for his family.

*   *   *   *   *

Enemy activity continued to be devoted to reconnaissance, with somewhat more aggressive fighter-tactics near the front. It varied with the weather, and as a result so did our patrols. About this time we devised a plan that enabled one flight to have a day off now and again. On these occasions we used to like to escape from our little village and organize a trip to Rouvres to see 73 Squadron, or to Nancy or Metz. Nancy was a particularly pleasant town, we thought—though possibly for different reasons. Usually we would have lunch together, and then walk round it in good spirits, talking and laughing, and exciting some interest as we passed by the crowds, mostly of women, in the busy streets. "Royale Air Force!" we would hear them say, or "C'est très jolie, cette couleur, n'est-ce-pas?" Usually the boys would like to go straight to the Roxy, of which more later, but I sometimes used to stroll about for a while in the old town, looking at the cathedral, at the Place Stanislas with its beautiful wrought-iron gates, and walking down the seventeenth-century chestnut avenue to the gothic Basilique de St. Êvre.

After my stroll, I would sometimes find it difficult to wrench myself back from the atmosphere of the Grand Siècle at its best, as perpetuated in the architecture of Nancy. But the atmosphere of the twentieth century at its worst, as typified by the Roxy, soon dispelled it, and by the time I had reached the top of the stairs and was handing my coat to the grinning cloakroom attendant, it was already well in the background, to be dissipated entirely as I walked through the doors of the bar. The transition was unpleasant, but the pain was fortunately quickly dulled by champagne. The room was low-ceilinged and softly lit, with a bar at one end and a dance floor at the other. Round the plush-draped walls were crowded tables and comfortable chairs, and round the bar was a throng of British and French Air Force officers, French Army officers, and pretty women waiting to be given a drink and a good time and anything else you liked. The dance-floor was crowded, and the air was filled with smoke and hot rhythm and a clamour of voices. After a drink or two, and a few exchanges with one's friends, one began to feel it was all quite jolly, and soon one would be laughing and chattering and dancing, and no doubt looking as damned silly as any of them to the casual observer (if there had been one). And so it went on, until at length Johnny would pull himself together with an effort and drag us out of the place an hour or so later than we'd meant to leave. We would be driven away by our driver (who would have had dinner at our expense by this time), and would next awake, tired, cold and rather fed-up, bumping down the hill into Neuville once more. We would draw up outside the Mairie, tumble out, call good-night to each other—and to our driver—and tramp off to our various billets to snatch a few hours' sleep before being awoken by the guard in the still cold hours of the morning to get up to the aerodrome again before dawn.

These expeditions abroad, so to speak, were infrequent, and varied with trips to Paris. The A.O.C., as a matter of fact, had expressed the wish that all his pilots should have 72 hours off in every 15 days. This was later reduced to 60. Actually it didn't work out as intended for us, for whereas the bomber boys had nothing in particular to do except sprinkle occasional pamphlets over the Siegfried Line at night, we unfortunate fighter pilots had to maintain a full Squadron (later reduced to a Flight of us and two of 73, and *vice versa* alternately) at Readiness or 15 minutes Available in all weathers. This, combined with the fact that the Bull (with his characteristic foresight) had sent everybody on Home Leave who could be spared in anticipation of a bust-up in the spring, gave those left behind little time off.

However, although I myself did not visit Paris after I was married at Christmas, we did manage to fit it in occasionally. If the form was anything like the pre-Christmas routine, the procedure consisted in a pleasantly anticipatory train journey (possibly helped along with a whisky-bottle); arrival at the Gare-St.-Lazare; a taxi along the busy, plebeian Grands Boulevards to (usually) the momentary quiet of a spacious room at the Crillon; and before-lunch drinks in the bar (champagne-cocktails, of course) following the luxury of a hot bath. These before-lunch drinks, unfortunately, had a habit of going round and round until about three o'clock, when the bar would shut. A hiatus would then occur—possibly employed usefully by walking round the shops—until five, when the bars reopened, and the after-effects of lunch-time could be nipped neatly in the bud.

Dinner *might* be a feature of the evening, but was fairly unlikely. Possibly we would finish up with a champagne supper in one of our rooms; or perhaps we would have drinks and supper with our friend Marjorie. She was a dress-designer, a Canadian, who kept open house for No. 1 Squadron and won us all by her generosity, her cheerful tolerance, and her interest in us. Marjorie was a great dear, and the C.O. made her the Squadron's first honorary member. From there we would perhaps crowd ourselves into a taxi and arrive with a rush and a roar at the Boeuf-sur-le-Toit, where we used to pay exorbitant sums for the doubtful privilege of sitting in the middle of a smoky room drinking more champagne, and only vaguely aware of the surrounding multitude of beautiful and curious women and the mixture of French Army officers, international pansies, crooks, bankers and spies, while Jack Wilson banged " We're goin' ter hang out the washing on the Siegfried Line " in a corner, first in French, and then in English, very obviously for our benefit. Then there would be an expectant lull in the conversation while we tried to sing and look whole-hearted about it. All the cafés shut at eleven, so it would be early to bed, and late to rise the next morning—but not too late to get quite-nicely-thank-you again by lunch-time.

Apart from organized trips, we used to manage to
amuse ourselves at intervals without going so far
afield. The various French units stationed round
about used to ask us over to dinner, and we used to
ask them back for drinks (which was all we could
arrange as a rule). At St. Dizier, a few miles south of
us, for instance, was a French Bomber-Reconnaissance
Squadron—the 1ère Escadrille, 33ème Groupe. This
Squadron was singled out for special mention by the
French High Command quite early on in the war, and
was at the same time honoured with two Croix de
Guerre and a Légion d'Honneur. To celebrate the
occasion, 1 Squadron was asked over to a special
dinner at St. Dizier.

As it happened, we were all feeling particularly cold,
tired and fed up on the evening in question, and in
any case only got about two hours' notice. We felt
that we would much sooner huddle round the fire and
then go to bed than turn out in the rain and have a
long cold drive in the buckboard. Consequently
there were no volunteers. As I more or less spoke
French, however, Johnny asked me if I'd mind going.
I felt it would be rather a bad show for only one of the
whole Squadron to turn up, and eventually I managed
to persuade Johnny, Killy and Boy to come along too.
We dashed off and spruced up, and eventually arrived
at the hotel at St. Dizier where the French Squadron
had their Mess.

We were feeling far from enthusiastic when we
trickled into the big mess-room, which had the usual
long table down the middle and a large bar at one end,
hung with the tricolour and the Squadron artist's very
passable efforts. However, after a formal presenta-
tion we were plied with champagne and introduced to
some quite comely and pleasant girls. Things looked
better already, thought Johnny and I, as we exchanged
glances. After more champagne and some dance-
music from the radio-gramophone the scene looked
positively agreeable, and we sat down to dinner
actually feeling quite gay. I sat next to Guy d'E——,

33

who spoke English slowly but well, and I am afraid I spent a considerable time rehearsing with him a speech I intended to make—for it was obvious that I would have to make one. Eventually the end of dinner came, and having fortified myself with a last gulp of champagne I rose to my feet.

There was silence. "Mesdames, mon Président, Messieurs," I said in the loud and, I hoped, clear tones befitting the occasion. "D'abord nous voulons vous remercier de tout votre acceuil. Nous voulons ensuite vous féliciter de la citation et des décorations que vous avez si courageusement gagnées, et nous sommes très heureux d'être ici ce soir et de célébrer cette grande occasion avec vous. De la part de la première Escadrille de Chasse de la Royal Air Force, je lève mon verre et souhaite ' Bonne chance ' a la première Escadrille du Trente-troisième Groupe de l'Armée de l'Air." Tremendous applause greeted these few words, and I sat down from my first public speech, gratified if embarrassed, to the roar of some peculiar phrase the company was shouting at me. " Pour vous, ça ! " said Guy; and I thanked him for his valuable co-operation.

Speeches were followed by songs, and eventually an English song was called for. We exchanged fearful glances. The English, I thought belatedly, are singularly ill-versed in the social graces. Then, on a silly inspiration that saved the situation, I rose to my feet again. Amid dead silence, and in serious tones, I said : " The English are a very musical race. And that is why we never sing. . . ." I sat down quickly, rather fearing I had missed it. But a momentary hesitation was followed by a roar of laughter that continued for some time.

After dinner we danced, drank more champagne, and danced again. Eventually, Johnny having been stood on his head and having finally passed out in the bottom of the car with Boy, we took our somewhat rowdy leave. The Wing Commander had gone home in his own car, and Squadron Leader P—— took us

34

back in his. All I can remember about the journey back was that it seemed extremely rapid, and that the following conversation took place :

" Not so fast, Paul," said P——.

" O.K.," said I.

Three minutes later.

" Ease off a bit, old boy," said P——.

" O.K.," said I.

Three minutes later.

" Hey, I'm not driving, you bloody fool, you are ! " I said.

" Am I ? " said P——.   " Oh, so I am ! "

    *   *   *   *   *

We were now in mid-April, and the weather was getting much warmer. The aerodrome, that had throughout the winter been an inhospitable place, alternating between soggy, muddy wetness and bleak, crackling ice, had now become very pleasant indeed. In fact, we practically lived up there, having our meals brought up on the buckboard and spending the time between patrols in basking in the sunshine. The only trouble was that the days were drawing out, which meant a pretty long spell of " Readiness " for us.

Enemy tactics had recently been showing a tendency towards experiment. All through the winter the German reconnaissance machines (the Dornier 17, Heinkel 111 and Junkers 88) had operated continuously but singly. They had paid, and continued to pay, particular attention to the area stretching west and north-west from " Hell-Fire Corner " (the corner of Luxembourg along the Franco-Luxembourg and Franco-Belgian borders). Sometimes these reconnaissance machines would pass the frontier in squadron formation, breaking up and dispersing on their different missions in the region of Thionville. The fighters for their part—the Me.109—had shown reluctance to cross the frontier or to engage our fighters. They evidently maintained a standing patrol on their own side, only crossing over to our side occasionally, and always very high. Now, however, the Luftwaffe began to come across in big formations; sometimes three squadrons of 109's would do a " sweep " as far as Metz and Nancy. The Me.110 had made its first appearance at the end of March, in close formation and very high, only engaging when pressed by our Hurricanes as previously related. To sum up, it was obvious that the Germans were trying out offensive tactics, and all in all, it looked very much as though the balloon might go up soon.

This thought caused us to pay even more attention than usual to our aircraft. Every pilot takes a pride in his machine, but the knowledge that he may be in action at any moment is an additional incentive. Accordingly there was a marked increase, in the Squadron, of interest in individual machines, and many hours were spent in flight-testing them, altering their rigging, adjusting the control wires to the tautness preferred by the pilot, getting the engine just so, harmonizing and checking the guns, testing them in the air, and in generally fiddling about and getting everything " on the top line." For the benefit of those who don't know, I should mention that the crew of a fighter aircraft does not consist solely of the pilot, although he is the only member of it who flies : the other two members, who are rankers, are just as important, and are known as the Fitter and the Rigger. The Fitter looks after the engine, the Rigger the airframe. The pilot depends on these two men, perhaps for his life. The Fitter and Rigger, on their side, are usually proud of their pilot and would do anything for him. Consequently there is a great spirit of teamwork and comradeship between the pilots, who are usually officers, and the men—not only the individual Fitters and Riggers, but all the men in the maintenance section, the armament section, and the flights themselves, even down to the A.C.H.'s, whose main task is to push the aircraft about on the ground. In my own Fitter and Rigger I had two fine men; I hope that they on their side had the same opinion of me that every crew has of its pilot. Much later, back in

36

England, I paid a visit to the old Squadron, especially to thank them for the work they had done for me during the French campaign.

*　　*　　*　　*　　*

In spite of the general atmosphere of impending trouble there was still time to appreciate the good things of life. The countryside was now in the full bloom of spring. Blossoming trees fringed the aerodrome; the grass took on a new greenness; the surrounding villages — Neuville, Revigny, Bussy —gleamed bright and clean in the sunlight; the barges on the canal, though always leisurely, moved through the lock more frequently; and the river that flowed past our village was so fresh and clear that one began to choose the places where one would soon bathe.

In this weather, on May 9th, Killy, Sammy (recently joined) and I got a day off and decided to go to Metz in Sammy's old Lagonda—I to see a girl called Germaine, who was a refugee with her family from a town on the German frontier. Arrived there, we parked at a café and found a table under the striped awning. It was pleasant to sit in the sun drinking our apéritifs and watching the passers-by : French officers, booted and spurred; officer-pilots of l'Armée de l'Air in their dark-blue uniforms, some wearing newly-won Croix de Guerre; Troupes de Forteresse from the Maginot Line in black bérets, their badges inscribed " On ne passe pas."

Towards evening Killy and Sammy, having appointed a place where we could meet later, made off on their unlawful occasions, and I went for a walk in the park with Germaine. We sat down on the soft turf of the bank of the Moselle and talked of many things. The evening shadows were lengthening, and the setting sun touched the turrets and spires of Metz with golden fingers.

Not suddenly, but gradually, a faint something intruded itself upon our peace. We stirred and looked at one another. Then the something came again, and

37

we became more aware of it—still not sure, but suspicious. A third time it came, and this time it grew : a rumbling, as of distant thunder.

"Les canons," Germaine said.

"No," I tried to reassure her. "I expect it's only practice bombing. There are a good many ranges round here."

But it was the guns all right, and heavy ones at that. Guns on the Maginot and Siegfried Lines. We jumped up and walked towards the town, thinking our own thoughts.

Back in Neuville, having said good-night to Killy and Sammy on the steps of the Mairie, I took a stroll up to the aerodrome. It was a perfect night, without a cloud in the sky, and the stars were bright and clear. There seemed to be a lot of aircraft about, though, and several passed over the village, the French anti-aircraft banging away furiously. They were lower than I'd ever known them before, too.

It remained noisy all night, and I slept restlessly. Several times I was awakened by the drone of aircraft and the sudden rending sound of A.A. shells bursting low overhead. Once a nosecap came whining through the air and hit the ground outside my window with a smack. I can usually sleep through these normal manifestations of warfare, but that night I tossed and turned, half-awake and half-dreaming. My dreams were of war, and the sounds of war in them kept merging into the real sounds outside.

I finally woke to find the guard entering my room. "Wanted on the 'drome immediately, sir," he announced. I cursed, rolled out, and looked at my watch—3.30. It was already light. I dressed and dashed along to the Mairie. Johnny and one or two others were waiting, and soon we were hanging all over the lorry that took us up on those occasions. Johnny rang up Ops. from the tent on the aerodrome and came out laughing. "C—— (the Operations officer at Wing) is in a hell of a stew," he said. "Plots all over the board."

38

At five the 'phone rang : " Patrol Metz, 20,000."
We steamed off, and were soon in formation and
clambering east. There was thick haze up to 5,000
feet, and although visibility above it was very good,
the ground was practically invisible. The low sun
made things worse, of course. The only features of
the landscape one could pick out at all from our
altitude were a few lakes and rivers, so finding our
patrol-line was not easy.

We could see no aircraft in the sky at all, and had
been droning up and down for some forty minutes,
feeling very fed up and hoping " B " Flight wouldn't
have all the luck, when over the R/T came, very
faintly and from another aircraft : " Enemy aircraft
going east from Ibor (Rouvres). Enemy aircraft
going east from Ibor. Hurry up for God's sake and
get the sods ! " We all woke up with a jerk and
closed in on Johnny, who swung away west. Soon
we saw something—a speck against the haze, miles
away and to the right, lower than we were and flying
on a course parallel with our own but in the opposite
direction. We opened up to full throttle, black
smoke pouring from our exhausts, and turned across
the aircraft's path. He was still some way off when
he saw us, and dived north. We gave chase, still not
quite certain of his identity. " Line astern—line
astern. Go ! " came from Johnny's quiet voice over
the R/T. Then as we got nearer and to one side :
" Yes—I think so—yes—yes, that's him ! No. 1
attack—No. 1 attack. Go ! "

Johnny was No. 1, Hilly No. 2, and I No. 3. We
watched Johnny go down, his little Hurricane looking
graceful but deadly, on to the still diving Hun—a
Dornier 215. We watched him open fire, but when
his incendiaries were finished couldn't see him firing.
We watched him gradually close the range to about
100 yards, then break away to the left and go down
in a steep glide. Looks as though he's hit ! Hilly
got on to the Hun next, and then it was my turn.
We were now only about 1,000 feet above the ground,

39

and the warm air was condensing on our cold wind-screens and forming ice on the inside : we had been scrubbing at them on the way down to clear them. I got in some good long bursts at close range, but things were made tricky by this ice, and also by the fact that the Hun was now right " on the deck," flying along valleys full of factory chimneys and skimming over thickly-wooded hills. I made room for someone else, and we attacked singly like this for another three minutes or so. The Hun did some magnificent flying and put up a jolly good show; it seemed almost a pity to smack him down now. I had seen no fire from his rear gun—probably Johnny or Hilly had killed the gunner. Eventually the Dornier slowed up so much that we had to zig-zag in order not to overshoot him. There were only three of us left by now—Hilly, Sgt. S—— and myself—and we hauled off and watched him. Obviously he was going to crash or forced-land. We saw him make a slow half-circuit round a large field and then go in to crash-land. He hit a ridge, bounced in the air, came down again and slithered along the ground, knocking off panels and bits of engine-cowling, and eventually came to rest.

We continued circling for five minutes, diving down to look at him, before anyone appeared. Some French soldiers at last strolled over from a nearby hamlet, and as they did so the roof of the Dornier's cockpit opened, and a figure stood up in it, waving both arms at us as we circled overhead. The figure then clambered on to the bullet-riddled wing and collapsed. The French took no notice of him, but fished down into the rear-gunner's seat to pull some-thing out—presumably the rear-gunner—whereupon Hilly and I turned for home (S—— had gone). I had no idea where we were—I had thought for a moment that we were in Germany, as a matter of fact, for we flew over a lot of trenches—and had no maps, so stuck to Hilly. A lot of aircraft were calling Ibor on the R/T for homing bearings, and one couldn't get a word in edgeways. Eventually, however,

Hilly got a bearing and arrived over Rouvres. Here I landed for petrol, but Hilly had plenty and went on.

While refuelling I had a chat with some of 73's boys. They had been busy, too, having been awakened by four Dorniers circling around the aerodrome at dawn at the unprecedented height of 3,000 feet. It was 73's day off, and they were all in bed, which was a pity, for they naturally took a very poor view of those Dorniers. They later brought a Heinkel down quite close to the aerodrome, and it exploded with such a roar that they suspected it was carrying bombs. This looked serious, for if it was the case it meant the balloon had gone up. Certainly it looked as though something was going on, for there had been several formations about, and probably the Dorniers that had circled Rouvres were looking for it, and either couldn't identify it in the haze or were carrying out a reconnaissance. Before leaving 73 I admired the effect of a Hun bullet that had struck the bullet-proof portion of a Hurricane's windscreen fair and square; it was just a big star now, far from transparent, but the bullet hadn't penetrated more than about a quarter of an inch before being flattened out : a comforting sight and fortunate for the pilot.

Back at Vassincourt, I taxied over to refuel and met a French officer of l'Armée de l'Air, with whom I had once had a very excellent dinner. He climbed up on my wing as I was about to taxi off, and said : "They have dropped bombs at Joinville, St. Dizier and Châlons-sur-Marne—on the railway stations!" I said "Les salauds!" or something to that effect, adding that we had just shot down one of them. I waved him good-bye, and as I taxied over to the dispersal point I wondered if his story was true. One heard such fantastic rumours at times. If it was, then the push for which we had been waiting for nine months had come. And yet . . . There had been so many scares, and nothing had happened for so long, that now one could scarcely believe it.

Back with the boys I learned that " B " Flight

had had a fight, Prosser having got a Dornier 17. Boy had apparently attacked his Dornier (the right-hand one of three) with such gusto that he only got a short burst in before over-shooting it and passing over the top. In doing so, of course, he presented a pretty target to the concentrated fire of all three Dorniers and got his aeroplane full of bullets for his trouble, one puncturing a tyre and another coming up through the floor, then through the right leg of his flying boot and overalls, finishing up finally in the boost-pressure gauge. Apparently it was Boy we had heard calling us up on the R/T and telling us about the Hun's position—though whether the one we saw was one of those attacked by " B " Flight is open to doubt. At any rate, we should not have sighted it had it not been for Boy's call.

Billy had apparently seen some Me.109's near Metz. He had somehow become separated from his section ; two 109's attacked him, but both pushed off after a bit of scrapping. Billy followed one and eventually got near enough to open fire. The Hun went right down to ground level at very high speed and streaked for Germany. Billy stuck to him well across the frontier, however, and to shake him off the Hun flew very low and eventually shot under some high-tension electric cables, hoping Billy would hit them. Not to be outdone, Billy followed under, caught the Hun up, and shot him down in flames in a wood, where he exploded. Nice work—if you can get it !

Well, it looked as though the war had definitely started. " Thank God ! " was the general feeling. " Now we'll get the damned thing over one way or the other "—but we thought our way.

I was very peckish and felt some lunch wouldn't be out of place. I was therefore rather startled to find it was only 9 o'clock ! We'd been up since 3.30 of course, but already it seemed as though we'd done a full morning's work. However, breakfast was as good as lunch, and we all set to when the buckboard arrived with it, and had a jolly good one.

Afterwards we sat about in the sun waiting for orders. As a matter of fact at that time we were only supposed to intercept bombing raids that might interfere with 73's move to Reims Champagne aerodrome. The French fighters were supposed to do all the protection, both of their own aerodromes and ours, and generally mess up the Hun bombers. Our rôle now was to cover the bombers of our own A.A.S.F.— the Battles and Blenheims—while they bombed the German advance on land.

We spent three hours waiting. There was nothing for us to do on the aerodrome except to sit, as usual, in the sun, which was by now pretty hot. The batmen were packing our stuff down in the village. We learned that 87's aerodrome had already been bombed and that they had been in action, though with what result we didn't know. Most of them had not been in action before, so we wished them luck. 73 had apparently been cracking all the morning, and had got some Huns. I have not given an account of all our combats, but pre-Blitz scores stood at : 1 Squadron, 26; 73 Squadron, 30.

At about 12 o'clock the 'phone rang and we were ordered to do our first bombing-cover, over the city of Luxembourg at 15,000 feet; to be there at a stated time and remain twenty minutes. " B " Flight were to do it, but someone was missing, so I asked to go. We had to get off right away because we hadn't much time, and naturally it was extremely important to synchronize our arrival over the target with that of our bombers. The Germans must be moving pretty fast if they were in the city of Luxembourg already, I thought.

Prosser was leading the show, of course, and the others were, I think, Boy, Billy, Lew, and Sgts. C—— and A——. I was detailed as " Arse-end Charlie." " Arse-end Charlie " was the one who did the guarding above and behind the main formation, which was usually in open Vic. His primary and essential job was to look after the formation's tail, which was " blind " when flying straight, to prevent surprise—and also, of course, to keep a general look-out behind. We had learned this technique from the French soon after our arrival in Eastern France, and usually had two " Charlies," who proved invaluable. In fact, never once during the whole of the French campaign was one of our formations surprised—though we were often attacked from above, which is a different matter; but we always saw the enemy before they were in range.

We set off. Haze was still present, though much thinner, and out of it rose growing, thermally-formed cumulus clouds. Being more or less detached from the formation, I could watch it as a whole from the side and on top. The five Hurricanes presented a picture that sent a thrill through me, though I had often seen it before. There was something graceful yet sturdy and venomous about them as they climbed, fast and straight as arrows, past the towering white clouds into the blue sky; something courageous and deadly in their sharp-nosed flight to battle, and something not without beauty.

We arrived over the city at the correct time. It lay far below us, just visible between the clouds. We were much too high to see any troop movements, and it looked much as when I had seen it—by accident— once before. We stayed circling, keeping our eyes very well skinned, and then turned, not entirely without relief, for home. We had expected a hot time of it, and had seen not a sausage. However, somewhere near the Luxembourg border we sighted a formation of fifteen Dorniers in sections line-astern and very fine close formation : they must have been a good squadron. We always looked above this sort of thing for trouble, and sure enough there it was—a squadron of Me.109's, split into two flights, in line-astern one on each side of the bombers, 3,000 feet above and slightly behind. Very nice. We were in a hopelessly inferior position to attack the fighters, being level with the bombers—which, incidentally, were

44

14   BATTLES SETTING OUT ON A JOB DURING THE BLITZ

15   BATTLES ON THE JOB: BOMBING A GERMAN CONVOY

16   A BLENHEIM RUNNING UP TO ITS TARGET

going N.E. and had probably dropped their dirt. If I had been leading the flight I think I should have tried to climb up to the fighters, probably with fatal consequences. But Prosser's experience did not desert him, and he called over the R/T "Leave them alone! Leave them alone!—do *not* attack!"

Just then we saw three other Hurricanes appear on the scene with a rush. Without looking to left or right, or, most important of all, above, they went straight in behind the bombers. We watched fascinated as one flight of six Messerschmitts came swooping down like hawks in line-astern. A second later a Hurricane burst into flames and went hurtling earthwards on its back. "My God! the bloody fools," we thought. The other two Hurricanes half-rolled smartly and beat it for all they were worth. In a few seconds the Messerschmitts had regained their height, using the speed of their dive.

We had naturally approached when we saw the Hurricanes attacked with a view to helping them out. Now we were right underneath the fighters, and both Messerschmitts and Hurricanes had rather broken up and were circling, they looking down at us and waiting for us to make a move to attack the Dorniers, and we looking up at them and hoping they wouldn't pounce, for they had all the height and outnumbered us two to one. However, Prosser called "Come on!—re-form!—re-form!"—and we did, and dived down and away in good order, with me snaking about like mad behind and developing eyes all over my head. A very neat and well-drilled little trap, that!

In parenthesis, I may say that our policy with regard to dealing with big formations of enemy machines had been decided on some time before May 10th. We had had, as the reader has seen, a certain amount of experience on the German frontier, and had made a regular practice of foregathering informally in the Mess to discuss tactics and determine our policy. After the Me.110's had appeared for the first time, we had had one such confab, at the end of which the Bull had said : " Well, to sum up, it seems probable that when the show starts the Hun bombers will have 110's and 109's above them. When we get cracking, *those* are the fellows to go for every time. Go for the top formation—and once you're in a fight, *don't* follow *anyone* who dives down or who is shot down. *Hang on to your height* and, of course, try and get above before attacking." That was clear enough, and summed up what we all thought. We liked to get these things fixed, because everyone's ideas about air fighting vary a little in detail, and if everyone carried out his own idea in combat the result would be lack of unity and discipline, leading to partial failure in one's object and heavy casualties through splitting up.

That our policy with regard to these escorted bombers was the right one in the circumstances I think everyone will agree. The ideal method of tackling these formations, of course, would have been for some of our fighters to have engaged and drawn off the enemy fighters, leaving others to tackle the bombers. But with the numbers at our disposal this could not be done, and we had to be content with endeavouring to achieve the first aim : that of drawing off the fighters, and leaving the bombers unprotected for any chance Allied fighters who came along. Very often, as it happened and as the reader will see, this policy was successful in turning a whole raid back. Presumably the Hun bombers were ordered to return if left without their escort—which was logical, of course, for they were poorly armed and fairly easy meat for a sufficient number of fighters.

Another point that I might make here is that the Squadron had developed, in the nine months preceding the Blitz, from an excellent peacetime team into a pretty formidable wartime combination. I do not write this boastfully at all. I mean that we all had a fair amount of war experience on top of considerable flying experience in peacetime; there was not one of us who was not capable of leading a section, for we all had done so; we knew every position in our formations;

and, above all, we knew each other's flying intimately, knew what we had to do in any normal circumstances, and knew what each one of us would be likely to do under abnormal ones. In short, we were a thoroughly trained and drilled team, each having confidence in the others, and most important of all, in the leaders. The value of all this may become apparent later on, though it should be obvious already.

Well, to proceed. After the Luxembourg affair, we were told to move to Berry-au-Bac as arranged. Wing had already left, and so had some of " B " Flight. When we arrived back at Vassincourt to hold the fort, the remainder of " B " Flight pushed off. We learnt later that on the way they ran across some Heinkel 111's, Boy shooting down one and Billy another. Lew, who was in another section, found himself a Dornier 17, and accounted for that, too. Good show.

Eventually we got the word to go. I flew in the Bull's section this time. We were soon over Berry, having seen many signs of bombing on the way. As we circled the aerodrome we saw a collection of bomb-craters where several sticks of anti-personnel (" that means *you* ! " I thought to myself with a curious shock) bombs had fallen near the Battles, one of which was " written off " (destroyed). We landed, parked our aircraft, and went over to the concrete huts where the boys were gathered, talking and laughing. We were feeling pretty tired by now, and as some of us had had no food since 9 a.m., were hungry. After a bit I lay down with my head on a pile of gravel underneath the larch trees. We had to hang around in case we were suddenly ordered off, though how this was to be done no one knew, the telephone to Wing not having been connected and the petrol tankers not yet having arrived to refuel our aircraft.

I lay on the ground and relaxed gratefully, stretched out in my dirty white overalls and flying boots, with my hands behind my head and my parachute and helmet beside me in case they should be wanted in a hurry. It was about four by now, but still damned hot. The

47

slender branches of the trees above me were laden with May bugs, and the bally things kept falling on me. In the distance was the sound of continuous bombing. I wondered how 73 were doing; their aerodrome at Reims Champagne had been bombed before their arrival, and all the dummy Hurricanes destroyed in a hangar. The sound of bombing became louder. War over France. . . . By contrast, an old peasant was harrowing the field a hundred yards away with a horse-drawn harrow. With him was a youth, his son perhaps, and in the same field another youth was harrowing with a fine team of horses. On a previous visit to Berry I had taken some photographs of them, and eventually, to please the lad, one of him standing with his horses, their brown muzzles over his shoulder. I had promised him a print, but hadn't yet been able to get it developed.

I dozed. I awoke to the sound of heavy bombing quite near and the drone of aircraft in the sky. The boys were peering up, and I jumped up and looked too. The sky was almost clear, with just a few little puffs of cloud. " There they are ! Turning—look ! " someone said. Yes, there they were ! About twenty bombers—Heinkels they looked like—turning away towards the east. But one didn't. " Look at this silly sod—what's he up to ? " said Leslie. We looked. He was coming straight over. " I expect he's doing a bombing-run—yes, did you see him correct then ? " I answered rather disinterestedly, remembering the days when I used to drop practice bombs from an Overstrand. " ***** " said Leslie, rather rudely. " Anyway," he added, by way of amplification, " I wouldn't move if a bomb dropped right there." He pointed to the ground 30 yards away. We craned our necks and shielded our eyes as the sun went behind a small cloud. Then we heard something. It began as a whisper, then increased to a faint whistle, rapidly rising to an unearthly shriek. One glance at each other, one look of realization on everyone's face, a few stumbling steps towards the concrete hut—then

48

17   THE MESS AT PONTAVERT, MAY, 1940

18   JOHNNY

19   HILLY

20   BELGIAN REFUGEES ON THE ROAD

21   MILITARY OBJECTIVE AT BERRY-AU-BAC

flat on our faces as the bombs burst with a series of air-splitting, deafening, terrifying crashes. I was beside a lorry, and I distinctly remember seeing the tyres leave the ground with each bang. Fragments pattered against it, against the hut. Then—stillness.

No one moved. I raised my head cautiously, expecting a scene of desolation and destruction. But no—there were the other boys, thank God, each similarly raising his head dazedly. Someone laughed, and we all got up laughing and wiping the sweat from our foreheads. " A bit close, those," remarked the Bull. " I've never seen Boy and Paul look so small ! " More laughter. " The bastard ! " shouted Leslie, summing up all our feelings, " What wouldn't I give to get that sod ! " Hilly was quieter. " Legitimate military objective," he remarked, as if to himself. He was right, of course. But funny to think that the difference of a hair's breadth and a split second to that German bomb-aimer would have accounted for No. 1 Squadron. . . .

Suddenly there was a faint shout from the field behind us, We turned and saw one of the boys who had been working in it staggering towards us. We ran over to him. His face was black with mud and dust and powder, his clothes torn and dishevelled, and he was just about all in. The bombs had fallen all round him, and how he escaped I don't know. We supported him, but he pointed across the field, saying, " They've got them ! They're over there—three of them ! " Against the wood we saw an indistinct heap. The bombs had dropped in two sticks—fourteen of them—starting on the fringe of the wood and extending to within 30 yards of where we had been. Among the craters and débris we found them. The old man lay face down, his body twisted and bleeding, one leg shattered, and a long deep gash across the back of his neck that oozed steadily into the earth. His son lay near, on his back and in a state I will not describe. Against the hedge I found the third boy—recognisable as having been a human being only by a few tattered

49

bits of clothing, a torn boot, and some splinters of bone. The five horses lay bleeding beside their smashed harrows; we shot them later. The air was still foul with the reek of high-explosive, and the bomber that had done it was scarcely out of sight, so quick had it all been. The boy who was with me pointed to the old man and said in a broken voice: " And he a father with eight children! " Then he turned and shook his fist in the air at the departing raiders, shouting passionately: " Oui, je te casse' la gueule, toi . . .! " I expect the German bomb-aimer, headed for his base at 15,000 feet, was entering in his log: " Military objective bombed at Berry-au-Bac—British aerodrome—Hits but no damage observed "; and the experts who would later examine the photographs taken at the time would just see a line of bursts, starting in a wood and ending beside a concrete hut.

*   *   *   *   *

That evening I did two more patrols—one over the aerodrome and another over Reims. Smoke was rising from several towns and villages: bombed. Reims Champagne aerodrome was full of craters: poor old 73 had had it all right. Here and there a farmhouse was burning, and the sight of the lazy red flames licking up made one feel slightly sick: it was all so thoroughly evil and hellish.

We landed in the evening, and though there was still an hour or two's daylight left, the Bull thought we had had enough for one day. So we piled into the bus and drove off, past the dead horses, past the cross at the cross-roads, down to little Pontavert, where we were billeted. We were tired, hungry and already overstrung, and after we had eaten and made the necessary arrangements for the morning, we went off thankfully to bed. My head had scarcely touched the pillow when I was asleep—having barely summoned the energy to say a prayer. So ended our first day of war.

We were up again at 2.45, refreshed by a sound sleep. We had to be on the aerodrome half an hour before dawn, so we grabbed a biscuit and a cup of tea in the Mess before going along.

The Bull had decided that our concrete hut made too good a target to be healthy. We guessed that the Hun bomber had been aiming at it on the previous evening, because from the air it was the obvious thing to try for; and considering that he was at 18,000 feet, his bombing had been damned good. Accordingly the Bull chose a place about 250 yards away on the fringe of the wood, and we spent the first few hours of daylight rigging up a tent there, into which we eventually had the telephone to Wing moved, together with a couple of desks, our flying kit, and so on. There were a shallow trench and a dug-out—also shallow—nearby that looked as though they might come in handy. They did. . . .

As the sun rose in the clear blue sky it got warmer, and soon quite hot. At about eight we got into our cockpits, for there seemed to be a lot of bombing going on. We sat ready and strapped in, gazing into the sky to the east, the troops sitting beside the starter-batteries on the ground. The idea was to get the aircraft off the ground and out of harm's way if a bombing raid came over, and perhaps to knock down a few bombers too. In this particular case " B " Flight were supposed to get off first and get after the Huns, " A " Flight then taking off and circling the aerodrome—or, of course, engaging if the chance came.

The aircraftsman on the ground beside me stood up and peered into the sky behind me. I had my helmet on and couldn't hear much, but even so I could detect a lot of crumps going off. I twisted round as far as my straps would let me and looked up. Yes, there was something up there all right; ack-ack shells were bursting all over the place. A " B " Flight engine suddenly burst into life down at the other end. I waved to the airman, and in a moment my prop was whirling in front of me and the machine shaking. As I waited for " B " Flight to get off I watched engine after engine start up. In a minute the first " B " Flight machine roared off across our noses, followed in quick succession by the other five.

I looked up to the right as my airman shook my aileron and pointed. Yes, there were the sods, turning away east again, at a good 15,000 feet. Soon I was off. There was no time to lose, no time to join up even, and I started clambering flat-out beside two " B " Flight machines—one of them with Billy's " P " on the side—after the Huns. They must have seen us take off, and we thought later that we had probably averted a heavy raid on the aerodrome, for they were now climbing at full throttle dead into the sun : good tactics. There were about a dozen of them—Heinkel 111's—in very open formation, presumably because they were flat-out. We were only catching them up very slowly, and it became apparent that if ever we did it would probably be over Berlin. Eventually one of the " B " Flight machines turned over and dived away back home, evidently in disappointed disgust. Billy kept on. It was obvious it wasn't much good now, so I looked around for something, maybe, within reach.

Sure enough I found it—over on the right, about 5 miles away and below me. I couldn't quite see what it was, but it stood out clearly against the top of the haze; and as I turned sharply towards it, it gave the clue to its identity by turning from its westerly course and diving steeply east, evidently having seen me, too. I nearly lost it in the haze, but soon got nearer and saw it was a Dornier 17. Having made quite sure, I attacked from astern. He was going bloody fast, and it was all I could do in my slow old wooden-blader to get within range. Long before I did so the Hun rear-gunner betrayed his feelings by loosing off wildly, the tracers flashing past me all over the place. I fired a short preliminary burst at long range, partly to put him off and partly to steady my aim, and having closed and got my sights on, I opened fire.

He started turning, first one way and then the other. The rear-gunner soon ceased firing. Realising that once he was on the deck shooting would be difficult, I fired longish bursts following each other as rapidly as possible. Soon he was right down on the trees, slowing up but still going pretty fast. Every time I fired I saw whitish smoke come from one engine or the other—presumably it was glycol—but the bloody man kept on flying and I ran out of ammunition. I must have got his oil system, too, for I got a lot of black oil on my windscreen.

I hauled off and watched him from above and one side. There was still no fire from the rear gun, but something that glowed like a Verey light came up towards me; I thought at the time it was a defiant shot from a Verey pistol, the gun being jammed, but I decided afterwards it was probably a French tracer-shell from the ground. Anyway, as soon as he saw me making no more attacks, the Hun turned half-right and flew straight due east. I did a roll over the top of him to wish him luck, and then left him, as he showed no signs of coming down now, and I didn't know where I was. If his engines lasted long enough without glycol and oil he probably made it all right, and I'm afraid I rather hope he did. Either my shooting was damned bad or he was full of armour, or both. Anyway, I felt he'd put up a better show than I had, and so figuratively raised my hat to him and departed.

I circled round uneasily for a few minutes trying to pick up my bearings. The country was very wooded and green. Luxembourg? Belgium? Somewhere round there, I thought. Fortunately I soon came to an aerodrome, with some Potez 63's round the edge; it was full of bomb-craters varying in diameter from six feet to sixty, as I found later. Since I was evidently in the right country, and was short of fuel, I parked down. Unfortunately, in trying to avoid the smaller bomb-holes, which were invisible at a distance as I ran along the ground, I swerved suddenly and dug my port wing in, bending up the tip.

I taxied over, wondering what the hell I was going to do about my aeroplane. The aerodrome was Mézières. I found the C.O. of the French squadron, who got an engineer to look at it. The engineer said it definitely couldn't fly, as engineers will. The ailerons still worked, though, and I thought it would fly with full right aileron. The C.O. left the decision to me, but said *he* wouldn't fly it. He said it might fly, but might do all sorts of things coming in to land. As he was a pilot of some 25 years' experience, I decided not to try.

The C.O. was a tall, hard-looking man, bristling with efficiency and perfectly undisturbed by the dozen or so delayed-action bombs scattered about the aerodrome. " Oh, those ! " he said. " Yes, they've been going off all night. One gets used to anything. . . ." His squadron was bomber-reconnaissance, co-operating with the French advanced light mechanised units in Luxembourg and Southern Belgium. They had not had many losses yet. " But," he added, shaking his head, " if *only* we had more fighters. . . ."

At my request he very kindly put an aircraft at my disposal to take me back to Berry, and having taken my maps and parachute out, I said *au revoir* to my poor old " G " with her red spinner. It was to be good-bye, and I still feel sentimentally sad about it ; for three days later Sammy took a lorry and a party of riggers out to see what could be done, and hadn't been there five minutes when there was a whine and a roar from the sky, and he had to lie in a ditch for two and a half hours whilst the aerodrome was wholeheartedly strafed by low-flying Dorniers. Sammy said he could actually see the pilots and gunners as they flew up and down a matter of a few yards away, bombing and machine gunning; and that they did their stuff beautifully, setting fire to all 15 Potez and various other aircraft on the aerodrome, and leaving the place unusable. Sammy's lorry was holed in two or three places; but, worst news of all to me, poor old "G" was riddled with bullets. I can only hope she was eventually burned before the Huns could lay their rude hands upon her.

Back with the Squadron, I didn't claim the Dornier, of course, though I entered it as a "possible" in my log-book. Wing had apparently kicked up a fuss about our taking off to chase up bombing-raids, and H.Q. at Reims pointed out that since we were there primarily to provide covers for our own bombers, how the blazes could we rush off all over the sky every time we saw an enemy one? So we were *not* —repeat *not*—to take off without orders, and if we saw a bombing-raid coming we were to lie down and lump it. All very well for them in their champagne-cellars, we thought. . . .

That afternoon we did a patrol over H.Q. at Reims. We were up an hour and a half, but saw nothing. Back at the aerodrome, "A" Flight dashed off to Pontavert for some tea. I had had no food that day and had been up since three, so I wasn't sorry. We swallowed the hot tea and bread and jam gratefully, and then steamed off again to the aerodrome as a message came through from Wing that a big formation of bombers was approaching Reims—45, they said!

Five minutes later we were off. Over the R/T came "Patrol Panther (H.Q. at Reims), height 10,000 feet," and off we went—Johnny leading, Hilly No. 2 on his right, myself No. 3 on the left, and Killy and Sgt. S—— 4 and 5 respectively and doing the cross-over behind. After about fifteen minutes over Reims, over the R/T came: "Two enemy aircraft going west from Sedan—two Dorniers going west; height, 5,000." We closed in and shot off to the north, rubbing our hands at the thought of two Dorniers to five Hurricanes.

As we approached Sedan, Johnny called: "There they are—there they are—straight ahead!" I couldn't see them at first, but suddenly I did, and my heart leaped. As we got nearer I counted them—30 Dorniers in two squadrons of 15 more or less in line abreast, covered by 15 Messerschmitt 110's in groups of twos and threes, wheeling and zig-zagging slowly above, ahead, beside, and behind the bombers. They were going west across our noses from right to left.

Johnny rocked his wings for us to close in more and went straight on, climbing a little to 7,000 feet, then turning left and diving towards them from astern. " Now keep in—keep in—and keep a bloody good look-out! " came steadily from Johnny. I glanced round several times as we approached to make sure we were not being attacked by something we hadn't seen, for the Huns still kept straight on although we were getting near. They must have seen us long before, but it was not until the last moment that the Me.110's wheeled, some to the right and some to the left, going into line-astern in their twos and threes.

We went in fast and in a tight bunch, each of us picking himself an adversary and manœuvring to get on his tail. I selected the rear one of two in line-astern who were turning tightly to the left. He broke away from his No. 1 when he had done a half-circle and steepened his turn, but I easily turned inside him, holding my fire until I was within 50 yards and then firing a shortish burst at three-quarters deflection. To my surprise a whole lot of bits flew off him—bits of engine-cowling and bits of his glass-house (hood) —and as I passed just over the top of him, still in my left-hand turn, I watched fascinated as he went into a spin, smoke pouring from him. I remember saying, " My God, how ghastly! " as his tail suddenly swivelled sideways and came right off, while flames poured over the fuselage. Then I saw, with relief, a little white parachute open beside it.

Good! I looked quickly around me. Scarcely half a minute had passed, yet as I looked I saw four other Huns going down—another with the tail off, a second in a spin, a third vertically in flames, and a fourth going up at 45 degrees in a left-hand stall-turn, with a little Hurricane on its tail and firing into its side, from which came a series of flashes and long, shooting, red flames. I shall never forget it. All the 110's at my level seemed to be hotly engaged, or about to be, so I looked around and above. Yes —those sods up there would be causing trouble soon! Three cunning lads were away from the fight, climbing all-out in line-astern to get over us and then pounce on the unwary. I had bags of ammunition left, so I immediately started clambering after them, with my " plug " (boost-override) pulled. They were in a slight right-hand turn, and as I climbed I looked around. There were three others over on the right coming towards me, but they were below. I reached the rear Hun of the three above and shot him down in flames in a couple of bursts. Then I dived at the three coming up from the right and fired a quick burst at the leader head-on.

I turned, but he was still there; so were the other two from above. In a moment I was in the centre of what seemed a mass of 110's, although there were in fact only five of them. I knew I hadn't the speed in my wooden-blader to dive away and beat it, so I decided to fight them and make the best of it. Although I was more manœuvrable at this height (6,000 feet), than the Huns, I found it impossible to get an astern shot in, because whenever I got one almost lined up, tracers would come shooting past from another on my tail. So all I could do was to keep twisting and turning, and when a Hun got behind me, do as tight a turn as possible, almost spinning, with full engine, and fly straight at him, firing a quick burst, and then pushing the stick forward and going underneath him. Then I would pull up in a steep climbing turn to meet the next comer.

Naturally they couldn't all attack at once without colliding, but several times I was at the apex of a cone formed by the cannons and machine guns of three of them. They used a lot of diving down and then

57

climbing up and taking a full deflection shot. Their shooting was wild, and this manœuvre was easily dealt with by turning towards them and going over their heads, causing them to steepen their climb until they were stalled and had to fall away. But don't imagine for a moment that I was enjoying this performance. Far from it. My mouth was becoming drier and drier, and I was getting more and more tired and desperate. Would they run out of ammunition? Would they push off? Would help come? I knew I couldn't hold out much longer.

After what seemed an age (actually it turned out to be fifteen minutes), I was flying down head-on at a Hun who was climbing towards me. We both fired— and then I thought I had left it too late and that we were going to collide. I pushed the stick forward violently and there was a stunning explosion right in front of me. For a moment my brain did not work. The aircraft seemed to be falling, all limp on the controls. Then, as black smoke poured out of the nose and enveloped the hood, and as a hot blast and a flicker of reflected flame came into the dark cockpit, I said to myself, " Come on, out you get ! "—pulled the pin out of my harness, wrenched open the hood, and hauled myself head first out to the right.

The wind pressed me tightly against the side of the aircraft, my legs still inside, and I remember catching hold of the trailing edge of the wing and heaving myself out. As I came free and somersaulted, it felt as though I was being whirled round and round through the air on the end of a piece of string by a giant. Then, as I fumbled for and pulled the ripcord, I was brought the right way up with a violent jerk that nearly knocked the breath from my body. My head was pressed forward by the back pad that had slipped up behind it, and I couldn't look up to see if my parachute was all right. There was no sensation of movement—just a slight wind as I swung gently to and fro—and for all I knew the thing might be on fire or not open properly. I heard the whirr of Hun engines as three of the 110's circled me, and as I looked at the ground I saw a shower of flaming sparks as something exploded in an orchard far below : presumably my late aeroplane. I heard the Hun engines fade and die in the distance, and rolled the rip-cord round the D-ring and put it in my pocket. I was still bloody frightened, for I was plumb over a wood and thought I would probably break my legs if I landed in it; and I confess without shame that I said several prayers, both of thanks and supplication, as I dangled in the air. Soon I was low enough to see my drift. It was towards a small village, and it looked as though I might clear the wood only to hit a roof. But no—it was the wood all right. I was now very low, still swinging gently, and saw two French motor-cycle troops running along the road, first one way and then the other. I waved to them. The trees rushed up at me. "Now for it!" I thought. I relaxed everything, shutting my eyes. There was a swish of branches, a bump as I did a back-somersault on the ground—and there I was. I had fallen between the trees.

I jumped up, and had scarcely done so when the two French soldiers I had seen on the road came running through the trees, one with a revolver in his hand and the other with a rifle. They stopped when they saw me, called " Haut les mains ! "—and stood pointing their weapons at me. I put up my hands and they advanced cautiously. I had white overalls over my uniform, and my helmet and oxygen mask were still on. I spoke through my mask with difficulty, and they wouldn't believe I was English. However, I eventually managed to persuade them to look beneath my overalls at my Royal Air Force wings, and they put up their guns and shook hands warmly.

I tore off my helmet and threw it on the ground, shouting, " Ces salauds de Boches ! " After that I felt better and calmer. We collected my parachute and went along to the village, I sitting in the sidecar of their motor-cycle combination. The whole village —Rumilly—had watched the fight, and had seen six Huns come down; they later found four more, making a total of ten. They saw me fighting the other five, and said it had gone on at least fifteen minutes, perhaps more. Later, when I got back to the Squadron, I found that Johnny claimed to have shot down one definitely and perhaps two, Hilly two, Killy two, and S—— two. With the two I claimed, that made exactly the number found—ten—leaving the number I had fought as five (total fifteen, as counted before the fight). The watchers on the ground had seen the tails come off two (one was mine and the other Killy's). I later got a fin off mine (it came down first), and with the black and white swastika on it, pierced by two bullets, it made a fitting match for the two last-war fins we had with the Black Cross emblems on them. Unfortunately the Messerschmitt fin was later abandoned, but not before I had got some pictures of it.

*　　*　　*　　*　　*

Donald (our equipment officer) came over to fetch me that evening in the Renault, but as we were late we decided to stay the night. We had an excellent dinner and drank a good deal. The French were enthusiastic over our victory, and I was very bucked to hear that the thirty Dorniers had turned and gone back when we tackled their escort.

We were awakened at dawn by the reverberations of very heavy bombing. We learnt later that Liart and Hirson, two neighbouring towns with railway junctions, had been flattened out with a heavy civilian death-roll. As one of the Frenchmen had said to me at dinner: " . . . il est fort, ce Boche ! "

We didn't get back to the Squadron till tea-time on the 12th, bringing in the fin in triumph. Killy told me he had seen me stuck with the Huns but could only say " Poor bastard ! " and beetle off, as he had no ammunition, and neither had anyone else. I felt it was my own fault for getting stuck, anyway. The aerodrome had twice been bombed since I'd been away. " B " Flight had had a fight, Leslie having got two Dornier 17's at Avaux, where he landed on a French aerodrome and was shot up by the ground defences. Prosser and Boy had each got a Me.110.

I now began to feel not so good. I had a hell of a headache, and felt jumpy and snappy. If anything disturbed me I felt like crying, and sometimes I could hardly speak for fear of bursting into tears. I thought perhaps the explosion in front of me (presumably a cannon-shell in the front tank) had concussed me slightly, for I had all the familiar symptoms of concussion. I was sitting on the steps of the verandah after tea with Boy and Prosser and one or two others. Boy said, " Come on Paul, let's have the story," and I surprised them and myself by snapping back, " What the bloody hell's the use of talking about it? "—then getting up and walking away. We were all a bit jumpy by this time, so my outburst didn't hurt anyone. But Boy came up as I stood moodily kicking the verandah rails, and said : " Look here, Paul old boy, I've never seen you like this before. Why don't you go and see the Doc? He'll fix you up." " Oh, I'm all right," I answered gruffly. " Spot of concussion, I think." But Boy persisted, and eventually I drew Doc B—— into a corner and explained things to him as best I could. He knew what the trouble was, of course (as a matter of fact, someone else was rather stricken, too). He said : " You go off to your room to bed, and stay there twenty-four hours. Don't say anything to the others. I'll see the C.O. I'll bring you a tablet, too, in case you can't sleep." Thank God we had a man like our Doc. He looked after us marvellously, and saved us many breakdowns.

Before I went, I learnt that some of the boys were going to Holland that evening to do a cover over Maastricht. I wasn't sorry not to be called upon to go, for I really didn't feel I could take it just at the moment.

As I walked up the sunny, dusty street to my billet, I glanced through aching eyes at the little war memorial, " Aux Morts de Pontavert." In my ears was the sound of intermittent bombing. My head was splitting, my emotions were almost beyond control, and I looked up into the brazen sky and wondered whether I could hang on, and if so for how long. I found the old woman of the house at my billet. She was glad to see me, having feared the worst. I told her I had escaped by parachute, and she said : " Well, you'll be all right now. You are destined to live." I wasn't convinced.

In my room I had a cold sponge down—and it was good to get the dust and oil and sweat of three days off my body. Then I closed the shutters and lay down, but I couldn't sleep. That damned bombing had me listening to it, and every time the A.A. guns behind the aerodrome fired I jumped up and threw open the shutters to look. I watched the white shell-bursts against the blue evening sky. I watched a Junkers 88 dive-bomb the aerodrome with heavy bombs; Hanks and some of the boys were in the dug-out and didn't like it, I learnt later : the bombs fell quite close. Eventually the Doc arrived and gave me a pill, and after some time I managed to get to sleep. Scarcely had I done so than I found my Hurricane rushing head-on at a Messerschmitt 110; and just as we were about to collide I woke up with a jerk that nearly threw me out of bed, in a cold sweat, my heart racing. I turned over and dropped off again—but the same thing happened. That went on at intervals of about ten minutes all the evening and all night, and I shall never forget how I clutched the bed-rail in an agony of fear. If there is ever a choice between physical and mental pain, give me physical every time.

At dawn I fell into a deep sleep, and learnt later that I had slept through two more bombing raids on the aerodrome. I got up soon after I awoke—at five on the evening of the 13th—and walked down the sunny street to the Mess feeling weak but rested, and unreal, as if in a dream. There was quite a bit of news. The Maastricht show had been pretty hot. The Bull had forced-landed in Belgium and was still missing; Lew had baled out on the wrong side of the lines and was now presumably a prisoner of war; Hilly had stopped two cannon-shells, but had got back all right. Leslie had got two Arados and a Me.109; Killy had got a Heinkel 112; S——, Lorry and Peter B—— (recently joined) each a Me.109. Subsequently we learnt that the Bull had got a Me.109 and an Arado, and Lew a Me.109, or possibly two. (It was on this occasion that the five Battles of 12 Squadron bombed the Maas bridges, " Judy " Garland getting a posthumous V.C., all five being shot down and only one gunner escaping alive. The bridges, however, were hit. Volunteers had been called for, and, of course, the whole Squadron had stepped forward.)

A few minutes after I had heard this the Bull rolled up unexpectedly in a Belgian car. He had made his forced-landing all right, and had seen some interesting sights in Belgium, among them four regiments of Senegalese going up to the front—at the trot, looking neither to right nor left, and with remorseless expressions on their faces. A Heinkel 111 had forced-landed in a field beside the road, and a section of these Senegalese troops had gone over to it, pulled out the four German occupants, and promptly decapitated the lot. They had then resumed their march, without a word or so much as a change of expression.

That day—the 13th—" B " Flight had been chasing something when Billy had called over the R/T something about oxygen and left the formation, presumably to go home. But nothing had been heard or seen of him since, and it didn't look too good.

As we stood chatting in the garden we heard some crumps not very far away. The aerodrome again, we thought, and we were right. A few minutes later we heard aeroplane engines, and were surprised to see a French machine of some sort—a twin with twin

63

rudders—flying low over the tree-tops past the village. "He's running from something," somebody said, "and he's asking to be shot down, too, flying like that." Then, as he passed by with a roar, we looked at each other. "Well I'm damned! If that wasn't a bloody Dornier I'll eat my hat!" "French markings, the sod!" "That means a bombing raid *here* to-morrow." "Well, blow me! Let's have another drink, anyway."

That evening we had all sorts of warnings from H.Q. about parachute troops : it was believed that they would try to seize our aerodrome and bump us all off in our village. Accordingly the Bull organized the aerodrome defences, ordered us all to sleep together and armed in the Mess, and informed us, the troops and the villagers that *anyone* seen off the road after dusk and before dawn would be shot instantly. During dinner he answered the 'phone and came back beaming. He told us that Lew had been taken prisoner by the Germans, but had been re-taken in the Belgian counter-attack. A cheer went up. Lew was already on his way to Maubeuge, apparently, where he would await our transport.

After dinner the Bull came over to me and said, "Look here, Paul, I want Lew collected as soon as possible. As I want Moses here, and you speak French decently, will you take the Renault over with O—— as driver and get off as soon as you can?" I said, "Right you are, sir," and rushed off to collect O——. It was 10.30 by the time we got off and just about to get dark. Refugees were already starting to stream through our village, though after dark the traffic slackened off a bit.

I was determined to reach Maubeuge, on the Belgian frontier, before dawn, for it was quite an important place from the point of view of communications, and I thought the Huns might bomb it at dawn—a favourite time. O—— was obviously getting tired —he nearly hit several unlighted carts—and besides, his eyesight wasn't as good as mine; so I gave him my automatic and took over the wheel, resolving to let him drive all the way back in the light whilst I slept. Maubeuge was a hell of a long way off, and we had to map-read, which wasn't too easy at night. Several times we nearly ran into unlighted military barriers and had brief arguments with the guards, who insisted that we should put out all our lights. Once a man stopped us and asked me the way somewhere : he had a car and was going wrong, so I put him right. " English ? " he asked, looking at my tin hat. I said that I was. " And speaking French without an accent ? " " No, I have a strong accent," I answered. He looked at me suspiciously, edging away, and I began to think he was a bit fishy, too. Anyway, we had no time for argument, so I called " Good-night " and drove on. One didn't know who was who those days. Everyone was suspect, and there was no check. Fifth Columnists and paratroops in all sorts of garb were known to be about. I didn't like it at all.

Soon we came to a " Route Balisée " (i.e., with small yellow lanterns along both sides, so designed as to be invisible from the air). Long convoys of lorries were streaming up towards Belgium, without lights and travelling fast. Some French guards made us, quite rightly, extinguish our lights, shouting " Les phares, bon sang—they've been bombing the road all night ! "

At last we arrived in Maubeuge. It was 4.30 and already light. I got the Commissaire Militaire out of bed with some difficulty. Yes, he had met the young Canadian, he had had dinner with him, but some French Air Force boys had taken him off to the hotel. Whereupon the Commissaire retired to bed again. I found the hotel. " No—no Royal Air Force officer. Never seen one." I tried another hotel with the same result. I returned to the Commissaire, who was sure he was in the hotel. Back there again I dragged the manager out of bed. No—definitely no English officer. I did the same at the only other hotel. Eventually I got fed up and declared that I was going to search both hotels from top to bottom, which I did, to find Lew snoring comfortably in bed. I hope I have since been forgiven for being such a nuisance, but the lethargy of those people was incredible. I suppose they weren't to know that every pilot we had was more than worth his weight in gold to us—and ultimately to them. To cut a long story short, we drove to the local aerodrome to collect Lew's flying kit (they had a standing-patrol of Moranes over the aerodrome, but didn't seem to bother about anything else), and drove back to Berry, I handing over halfway when I started falling asleep. We left Maubeuge at 6.30 and got back to the Mess at Pontavert at lunch-time.

There was still no news of Billy. I remember going into his room after lunch to get something, and seeing his small personal possessions spread about, as I had seen the personal possessions of many another Air Force comrade in similar circumstances—a photograph of his mother; a bottle of hair-oil; the pyjamas that he would perhaps need no more. Poor old Billy!

Shortly afterwards I was called to the 'phone by Squadron Leader P—— from Wing. He said: "There's a message from the hospital at Rethel to say they have an English officer-pilot there, and we think it may be Billy. Will you go out to see?" I was dog-tired, all the good of my previous day's rest having been undone, but naturally I said "Yes, sir," got the Bull's permission, and rushed off again.

The roads were getting more refugee-traffic every moment, mostly cars from Belgium, Luxembourg, and the Sedan district, but we made good speed and got there at about four. There was a lot of droning in the sky, and the inhabitants were taking cover. We crossed the railway and went up a steep hill to the hospital. Ack-ack guns were firing not far away, and bombs were dropping somewhere. I left O—— in a courtyard, telling him to take cover, and walked along to another part of the hospital where "le pilote

66

anglais " was laid up. I found him in a room with a French officer—and, by God ! it *was* Billy ! He was lying half on his stomach, having been operated on that morning. He told me that, having no oxygen, he had had to leave the flight. On the way back he saw four Dorniers and attacked them without having seen any escort. He got one Dornier, and perhaps two, but a moment afterwards he was shot up to glory by Me.110's from behind, getting two bullets in the leg, one in the back, and a lot of cannon-shell splinters in his back, too. His aircraft caught fire and he baled out. He passed out on the way down, but came to soon afterwards to find tracers whistling past him from the 110's. As he heard a hell of a battle going on overhead, however, it is quite possible that that was where the bullets were coming from. He didn't feel so good now, and spoke haltingly and with difficulty.

As we talked there was the father of bangs just outside the window, and the French nursing orderlies started hopping about and ducking behind things. I said, " What the hell's that ? " and Billy answered, " Oh, don't take any notice—it's been going on all day." So, while bang after bang shook the ward, we went on talking as calmly as possible. After all, one had to set an example. The Frenchman in the next bed was also a pilot, and was badly burnt and knocked about, having had a nasty smack-up. He was almost in tears, poor bastard. I took a list from Billy of things he wanted sent along—toilet articles and so on, and the pyjamas he *did* need after all. Then I left him and went out into the hot sunlight.

What perfect weather it was ! I found the banging was caused, not by bombs as I had thought, but by an ack-ack gun just beside the hospital. Everyone was sheltering in caves in the side of the hill, some standing in the entrances and gazing up at the shoals of German bombers going over westwards. They called to me to take cover, but I wasn't going to risk having my transport bombed and being stuck there. I found

O—— waiting in a doorway. We jumped in and drove down through the town and over the level-crossing beside the station. Bombs were falling somewhere near, and everyone was running to shelter or gazing into the sky. Refugees were lined up beside the road, and as we passed they waved to us to stop and pointed up. I said, " Step on it, we're going to give that railway line a bit of a margin ! " and we shot up the straight tree-lined road.

A quarter of a mile out we pulled up abruptly under a tree hard into the side. We jumped out, and I told the driver to get down the banking and lie down, meanwhile shouting to all the refugees within earshot to do the same. The poor devils were just standing along the roadside gaping up at the sky, whence came the dull roar of many engines. I got a lot of them down the banking, and was glad to see the others all down the road following suit. I then ran down myself, helping an elderly woman and her son and daughter, with the latter's child. I showed them how to protect their heads with their arms whilst flattening themselves on the ground : they had to be told everything. When the bombs started to fall I even had to shout at them to make them keep down; they seemed stunned, and unable to realize at all what was happening.

I watched 25 Heinkels go straight overhead at 15,000 feet, returning in sections echelon starboard a few minutes later. As we lay flat, stick after stick of H.E.'s came whistling down, bursting with crackling roars on the station, the railway, across the road, and in the surrounding fields. Eventually it was over, and as the drone of the engines died away in the distance I told the refugees it was all right, bade them good-bye and good luck, and ran up on to the road with O——. Across the fields the station was in flames. A pall of dust hung in the air all around, drifting slowly away in the slight breeze. In the curious silence the refugees trickled slowly back to their pitiful carts and bicycles. The nearest stick of

68

bombs had dropped 30 yards from us. I hoped Billy was all right—the town didn't seem to have suffered. It was beautiful bombing. . . .

On the way back we stopped and listened before entering each town. We passed Reims Champagne aerodrome : there seemed to be a lot of holes in it. At last we reached Pontavert. I thought probably poor little Pontavert would be wiped out soon. " Il est fort, ce Boche . . . ! "

Donald dealt with Billy's list, but he never took the things to Rethel because the hospital was evacuated next day. The town was subsequently blasted off the map.

*   *   *   *   *

I heard quite a bit of news at supper—which consisted, incidentally, of a magnificent salmon presented by Madame Jean to Donald and Knackers when they had gone over to Bar-le-Duc the previous day to pay our bills and so on. On the way they had passed through Châlons, which was absolutely in ruins. Revigny had had it badly, too, but Vassincourt aerodrome and Bar-le-Duc were as yet untouched. There was some talk of our going back to Vassincourt. Curiously, that aerodrome was never bombed. Our own at Berry had been bombed again that evening : they had seemed to aim at the fringe of the wood, presumably because the Battles used to be dispersed along it. " B " Flight had had another fight with a big escorted bomber formation : Boy had got a Me.110 and a Heinkel 111; Prosser, Lorry, and G—— (recently joined) a Heinkel 111 between them (Lorry had to force-land with a bullet in his engine, getting out just before his Hurricane went up in flames on the ground); Leslie had got a Me.110 and had attacked two Heinkel 111's, shooting one down and landing beside it. The machine had forced-landed and the pilot was beating it, but Leslie chased him and brought him down with a low tackle, later handing him over

69

to the French, but not before he had availed himself of the Hun's Mauser automatic.

Sammy had been to Mézières to see my aeroplane, as I have told elsewhere. On the way back, not far from Rethel, he had seen a magnificent fight between six Hurricanes and a dozen Me.110's. They were right down at about 1,000 feet at the end, and Sammy had to lie in a ditch to avoid the machine-gun bullets and cannon-shells that were pinging and banging all over the place. He said that if he'd had a movie-camera he could have got some shots that would have made " Hell's Angels " look like something out of a Sunday school sequence. We miss half the fun in the air. . . . Sammy saw several 110's come down in flames with a roar and a bang, and a couple of Hurricanes, too. The last Hurricane to leave the scene had evidently run out of ammunition, for it had to dodge in and out of the trees with a 110 on its tail before eventually getting away. The Messerschmitts—what was left of them—pushed off then, and Sammy ran over to where one of the Hurricane pilots was dangling in his parachute from a tree. He was in a nasty mess— covered in blood and badly burnt—and was scarcely recognizable as " Fanny " O—— of 73 Squadron. The other Hurricane pilot was killed—we never heard who he was. Fanny got a couple of 110's in this fight before being knocked down; his total score was now 18. " A " Flight had also had a fight, having run into some Junkers 87's—the answer to the fighter-pilot's prayer, but the only ones we ever met—escorted by Me.109's. Hilly got a Me.109 and a Ju.87, Stratters a Ju.87, Sgt. C—— a Ju.87, Pussy a Me.109, and Sgt. S—— a Me.109. Again no one lost: it seemed miraculous—so far.

Our nerves, though, were getting a bit frayed by this time, and we were very jumpy and morose. Few of the boys smiled now, and we were no longer the cheerful crowd we used to be. But we could still laugh occasionally, as when we heard a broadcast on the nine o'clock news made by the B.B.C. observer at

Reims, during a bombing raid; or when we heard, also on the news, Leslie's tale about chasing the Hun on the ground.

We heard the news, too, that the Luftwaffe had been ordered to " harass " refugees. We hoped we'd catch some of them at it. We never did, but that very evening we found ample evidence that the order was being executed, for refugees were streaming through our village. Sammy, Boy and I piled Sammy's car with food collected from the cookhouse, the mess and the store-room—bread, bully beef, jam, etc.—and distributed two car loads (which was all we could spare) to the unfortunate people. They told me that *this* little girl had had her father killed by a machine-gun bullet from a " strafing " Hun, that *that* young woman had had her child's brains smashed out by a bomb-splinter, and so on. It was heart-breaking to see these poor people, hungry, tired, with the light of fear in their eyes, fleeing before the Nazi scourge. They were becoming a definite menace to our own forces by blocking communications, and were being deliberately and ruthlessly used by the Germans as an army under the lash of the Luftwaffe. We had started fair-mindedly by making full allowance for all alleged German atrocities; in fact, we had complained more at the fact that the Germans had made war at all than at their methods of waging it. But as time went on, and they gradually gained the upper hand, they definitely became more and more ruthless and cruel— in other words, as reprisals became less likely. I suppose their argument was that by killing a few thousand refugees they would shorten the war and ultimately save many lives; but could *you* machine-gun and bomb helpless old men and women and children under *any* circumstances? Could any human being worthy of the name? Johnny's way of describing them was not poetic, but it hit the nail on the head. He said: " You know, there's no getting away from it—they *are* * * * * s, aren't they? "

*   *   *   *   *

71

The morning of the 15th dawned clear again; the Germans had certainly made no mistake in their meteorological department. We had been expecting parachute troops at dawn, so we were all up and about at 2.45 again. It was "B" Flight's early turn. Shortly after dawn some heavy bombs were dropped on the aerodrome. Poor old "B" Flight always seemed to get the bombing! We relieved them at eight so that they could get some breakfast.

It was hot on the aerodrome. Enemy air activity was in full swing again, and the sound of bombing was almost continuously in our ears. There was nothing to do but hang around, or now and then go and check the sights on our aircraft that had just been harmonized. At about 11.30, "A" Flight was sent off to do a patrol over Reims at 10,000 feet. We hadn't been there more than ten minutes when over the R/T we heard P——'s voice from Wing saying: "Much air activity near Vouziers—very many Huns near Vouziers." We closed in and swung away north-east.

After five minutes Johnny said: "God! Close in—close in!"—and we saw them. There were about 40 Dorniers in close formation at 10,000 feet, and above them squadron after squadron of Me.110's stepped right up to 18,000 feet. I counted about 80 110's, and then gave it up, for everywhere one looked one saw another squadron. They were coming straight towards us, and Johnny led us to the left, climbing as hard as we could. As we skirted round their right flank Johnny turned towards one of the squadrons of Messerschmitts at about 16,000 feet, saying, "Here we go—now keep a bloody good look out!" Fortunately I was doing so, and saw another squadron about 2,000 feet above and behind as we were going in astern of the first squadron. I gave a shout over the R/T to indicate what I had seen. Johnny answered "O.K., Red 3—O.K.," and we swerved away and climbed up flat-out.

The 110's saw us as we reached their level astern of

them—they may have seen us before, but they seldom broke formation until attacked. They immediately formed a defensive circle, flying round and round one behind the other. I lost sight of the others, and climbed above the circle. Then I selected a Messerschmitt, and dived on him from above, finishing in a sort of quarter attack. There seemed to be a lot of fire from the 110s' rear guns all round the circle, but I wasn't hit, and held fire till I could give my Messerschmitt a long burst close in. A lot of bits flew off him and flames leapt from his engines. I had time to see him go into a vertical dive as I pulled up violently to avoid being caught by his comrade behind him, but the air now seemed to be full of Huns, and I had to switch my attention over to them.

Another squadron seemed to have joined in. I am not sure whether the circle broke, but looking back on it, it would seem that the squadron attacked went into a defensive circle to engage our attention while another squadron attacked us. Anyway, I saw a Hurricane below me being attacked by a Hun, and dived on his tail. The Hun pulled up at about 60 degrees with me still behind him and firing long bursts savagely into him. Smoke suddenly poured from him and he fell away to the left with little flames shooting down his fuselage. I couldn't watch him further, because just then I heard " Pop-pop— Bang ! "—and swerved to the right to see a 110 coming straight up behind me, firing for all he was worth. I saw a large cannon-shell hole in my port wing, and several bullet holes. A thin trail of whitish smoke was coming out from underneath my nose, and I said to myself, " This is where I leave ! "

I half-rolled violently to the left, went straight under the 110's nose, and then dived vertically for the ground at full throttle and in maximum revs., aileron turning on the way down. What speed I was doing at the bottom of my dive I don't know, but it must have been bloody fast, for I came down from 18,000 feet. As a matter of fact, I had a bit of a job pulling out, but I did so in a gentle turn, using my tail-wheel carefully and glancing behind. I went right down to ground level before levelling off completely. Smoke was still pouring from my nose, and I guessed an incendiary had found the glycol-tank and set fire to it. There was no one behind, thank the Lord, so I pulled up to 1,500 feet, throttled back to 170 m.p.h., reduced revs., and set a south-westerly course. I had no maps, but I remembered we'd flown north-east to Vouziers. The smoke didn't seem to be getting much worse, though it still poured out steadily. I was flying a nice new Rotol, and I hoped to get it back more or less in one piece, providing the fire didn't spread and catch the petrol. I didn't want to force-land, because I thought the thing might go up low down, or explode on the ground, so I opened the hood, undid my oxygen-tube, and had everything ready to bale out, with the aircraft trimmed slightly nose-down so that the tail would go up as I went out and I wouldn't hit it. I meant to do it in style this time!

Actually I did it in damned bad style. The smoke suddenly increased and turned grey, then completely enveloped the nose and the cockpit. I let go of the stick to dive out, but naturally as I did so the tail went up (it being trimmed to do so) and I was shot straight up into the air and over it. I was so surprised to find myself in a state of suspension in space that I very nearly forgot to pull the rip-cord! As I was low down this might have been serious, but I woke up with a curse and pulled the thing so enthusiastically that I ripped off a couple of finger-nails, which was annoying.

I saw my aircraft go down in a long curving stream of grey smoke, and explode with a dull " boom " in a field. I just had time to roll the rip-cord up and put it in my pocket, hoping to God I wasn't going to land on a barbed-wire fence I could see below, when I was almost on the ground, and swinging violently. I hit it with a hell of bang on a down swing, doing a couple of somersaults. There was a lot of droning overhead,

74

and I didn't want to be ground-strafed, so I jumped up and gathered up my white parachute, hiding it under a tree beside the barbed-wire fence.

I looked around. A couple of fields away I saw a French peasant with a rifle running towards me. To the other side, across the barbed-wire fence, was a sort of swamp with a small stream running down the middle of it, and on the other side of that a road, along which I saw a Royal Air Force car racing. As it drew level I waved my arms and it stopped abruptly. A tender following behind also stopped, and a posse of airmen, armed to the teeth, leapt out and advanced in very nice open order to the far edge of the swamp. I shouted across: "It's all right—I'm British!" Some officers appeared from the car and called, "Come on over, then!" Just then the Frenchman behind took a pot at me, but I wasn't particularly interested in him and just waved to him as I climbed the fence with my parachute. I got soaked to the top of my thighs wading through the swamp and the stream, but it was a warm day—and besides, I felt quite pleased with life.

As we all shook hands (I used my left because of my lost finger-nails) there was a roar from an aerodrome about half a mile away, and a column of smoke and dust rose high in the air. "There goes one of our bombed-up Battles," said one of the officers—the Germans were bombing Amifontaine aerodrome. They took me along to 75 Wing H.Q. in Amifontaine village, where I was given a very good and welcome lunch. The few officers present seemed to think I was taking things very calmly, but I really saw nothing to be much disturbed about. I had got over my first experience of "brolly-hopping"; this second effort had been perfectly straightforward, with plenty of time for preparation, and I had honestly rather enjoyed it.

One of the first things I had done on entering the Mess, of course, was to ring up "Panther" (Reims H.Q.) and tell them that I was safe and to let my squadron know. A curious thing was that when they asked, " Did you get any Huns? " I said " No, I don't think so." The fact was I just couldn't remember a single detail of the fight until some hours later. This is by no means an unusual occurrence, and is a strong argument against putting in immediate combat reports.

After lunch I said good-bye to my hosts and thanked them for their hospitality. They gave me transport to Reims, which was nearby, where my own transport would await me at the " Lion d'Or." It was there on my arrival, and I took my two drivers in for a drink. Inside I met some of the 73 boys— " Ginger," " Cobber," and one or two others. We had a few " coupes " of champagne and swapped news. Cobber told me he had sighted a lone Dornier that morning, but before he had even got within range the whole crew had suddenly baled out!

Arrived at Pontavert once more, I found some of the boys having tea in the Mess. They laughed when I said : " Shot down again, sod it ! " and asked all about it. Apparently we had knocked down a few in the fight, Johnny having got a 110, Killy one, S—— one, and C—— one; I claimed one and one probable, and as they subsequently found six or seven lying about the countryside in varying stages of disintegration, presumably my probable came down. Johnny had again stopped a bullet in the engine from the rear gun of a 110 he had chased down to ground-level; as he was going straight for a belt of high trees when his engine cut out, things were a bit tricky for a moment, but he managed to clear the trees by inches and put the machine down in a field with the wheels up. He had been brought back a short time before in a French motor-cycle combination looking most annoyed ! The Bull gave me a bit of a raspberry (quite rightly, I now thought) for trying to fly a burning aeroplane back. He said : " I don't care a damn about losing an aeroplane—there are plenty more of those—but I do care about losing you, or any of my pilots. Next time, Paul—out straight away."

The 'phone rang, and news came through that " B " Flight were off, so we piled into the buckboard and rushed along to the aerodrome. Apparently a large formation of Me.110's had flown across it at 15,000 feet, while Laon was being heavily bombed. Presumably this bombing was successful, for we could see that one of the long, fast French convoys that roared continuously along the Reims-Laon road was now stationary. " B " Flight had not been ordered off, but a little " B " Flight fitter had come running up to Prosser and said : " Come on sir ! Do get up and into 'em ! Come on, sir ! " Prosser shook his head and said : " No—it's no use now—we'd never catch them at that height." But the little fitter said : " Oh, come on sir ! No. 1 Squadron's not going to let the cheeky sods get away with that ! Come on, sir ! I'll start all the bleeding kites up by myself if you'll go ! No. 1 Squadron, sir ! " Prosser looked at Boy and Leslie and Lorry ; they nodded, and off they all ran to their machines, much to the little fitter's joy. Just before they took off a formation of Heinkels had come over and bombed the aerodrome. The troops, who had all along behaved magnificently, never flinched, and went on strapping in the pilots and starting up the machines as the bombs came whistling down. The Flight took off through a hail of bombs that burst all over the aerodrome. They were still up, so presumably they had engaged.

Eventually Boy came back, alone—we knew it was Boy by the " T " on his aircraft. He circled carefully, looking for a clear run through the bomb craters, and then parked down and came in. We walked over to him as he climbed out, and as we examined some fresh bullet-holes in his machine he told us that they had caught the Messerschmitts (30 of them) because they had turned and come back. He had got two and run out of ammunition. Unfortunately some of the 110's were still paying him a good deal of atten-

77

tion, and he had a hell of a time getting away. He went right down to ground-level with a couple of Huns on his tail, and it took him some time twisting and turning through trees and other obstructions to shake them off. "What my poor bloody engine's like I don't know," he said. "I've honestly never been so scared in my life! Whew!"

Prosser, Leslie and Lorry were still missing : Wing knew nothing about them. However, no doubt they would show up in due course. Soon Wing had mercy on us and told us we could go off to the Mess and relax, which we did with gratitude.

We hadn't been there long when a message came through to say that Prosser had baled out but was safe and on his way to us. He arrived soon after, alternately cursing and laughing because his trousers were soaked from top to bottom in foul, sticky glycol, which never dries out. His eyes were inflamed, red and bleary—also from glycol. We laughed when we saw him, and asked for his story. "Well," he said, "it was damn' silly. To start with, I only took off because of that bloody fitter, and knew that we'd never catch the sods. But they turned, and so we did. We got above them, and I dived vertically on the leader and fired a burst, allowing deflection, and he just blew up. Nothing left of him but a few small pieces. Then I pulled up in a climbing turn to the left and saw a bastard coming up at right angles towards me from the left and firing He wasn't allowing enough deflection and all his shots were going behind me. I was just turning over him and laughing at him like hell when my aeroplane was hit by some other sod behind and I was suddenly drenched in hot glycol. I didn't have my goggles down and the bloody stuff completely blinded me. It hurt like hell! I didn't know where the hell I was then, and somehow I got into a spin. I could see damn-all and the cockpit was getting bloody hot, so I undid the straps and opened the hood to get out, but I couldn't. Every time I tried I was pressed back. I started to

scream then, but somehow or other I stopped screaming and then I got out. I came down all right.
That's all. Now let's have a bloody drink."

Over our noggins we discussed the general situation, of which there had been little time to think until
now. There were reports that the Germans had
broken through at Sedan; others suggested they had
been let through for strategic reasons. The Bull told
us there was talk of a " strategic withdrawal," and
that we might be moving soon. Wing had been
bombed. We thought it certain that the Germans
knew we were in Pontavert, and we had been warned
once more about paratroops. The Bull had organised
a special guard on the aerodrome to look after the
machines, and had again decreed that we were to
sleep in the Mess together, with our revolvers near at
hand. We thought it crazy at the time, but he was
right.

Sammy, Killy and I had a talk on tactics. It started
by Killy's saying, " I hope Leslie and Lorry are all
right. It seems funny we haven't heard of them,
because the fight was only a few miles away, and they
must have come down somewhere near." I shook
my head and said, " It won't surprise me if Leslie's
gone. He's been rushing about the sky like a mad-
man for the last five days. He's too inclined to rush
into these bloody Huns." Killy said, " I've been
rather thinking the same thing about you, as a matter
of fact." Sammy said, " Yes, you don't want to
overdo it. Look at the blokes who got big scores
last time—Bishop, Mannock, Richthofen; they only
got away with it because they always chose
the moment to fight and the moment not to fight.
They often refused combat." I said, " My own
personal view has always been : attack, attack, always
attack, no matter what the odds or the position, and
go on fighting to the end if necessary. But now I
must say I'm beginning to modify my views a little.
This thing's obviously going on for a hell of a time,
and perhaps one serves one's country best by not

79

throwing one's life away carelessly. As a matter of fact, the main reason I broke off that fight to-day was because I *have* changed my ideas a bit. A few days ago I would have gone on fighting even with the glycol on fire, and probably have been bumped off."

We all agreed that, although we were tired out already, the Huns wouldn't be able to keep up this pace long. They seemed to be having things too much their own way, though, and to have anticipated more opposition than they got, for they were now coming over in very slovenly formations, and often without escort. I must say we wondered what the bloody hell the French fighter squadrons were doing. They had shot down 75 Huns on the first day, but we hadn't seen a single French fighter in the air since May 10th, although we had seen many sitting on the ground, cunningly concealed round well-camouflaged aerodromes. The sky is a big place, of course, but we'd seen a good many Huns in it. Meanwhile, the Luftwaffe was systematically, and practically without opposition, destroying aerodrome after aerodrome, railway junction after railway junction, town after town—and, significantly, no road bridges. Obviously the Hun was blasting a path for his army. This rumoured " strategic withdrawal " looked a bit fishy to us.

After supper a French colonel suddenly appeared in the garden. No one took much notice of him and he naturally looked a bit annoyed, so I went up and asked him what I could do for him. Apparently his car had broken down in the village. Could we mend it? He looked cross when I asked him for his identity card, but he produced it. I was as polite as possible, but he wasn't very responsive. I got a fitter to look at the car : the starter was jammed, the spring being broken. He had his wife in the car, and a lot of luggage, and said he was taking her to Paris. She was nice if a bit stupid—he was stupid, too. They declined my offer of tea or a drink in the Mess, but melted a little. The fitter worked on as we stood by the roadside. A French poilu came up, saluted the Colonel, and asked, " Can you please tell me where the such-and-such infantry regiment has gone, sir? I was asleep in my billet and they left me behind at so-and-so." (I didn't catch the name.) The colonel said he didn't know, but thought they were at a particular spot. I tried to catch his eye while the man asked several more questions, and when he had gone respectfully suggested that it would have been as well to investigate his identity before answering questions on military dispositions. The colonel, however, was gruffly disinterested, and waved his hand to dismiss the subject. The car was nearly fixed. I wondered how even a French colonel could take leave at such a moment, but at the same time I was glad he was getting his meek little wife out of it.

The ever-present sound of distant bombing grew suddenly nearer, and we could hear the long, melancholy sighing of whistling bombs. It wasn't the ear-splitting, terrifying shriek that whistlers make when they are falling on you, but a sort of low, menacing moan, an evil echo in the sky. Reims again, I thought. Soon a big formation of bombers came droning over the village, going east, presumably on their return trip. I wondered if they would at last flatten out little Pontavert. I told the colonel and his wife to throw themselves in the ditch if they heard bombs coming, or if I shouted to them. There were some small cumulus clouds, about 3/10, at 3,000 feet, and we stood peering up between them into the clear evening sky above.

Suddenly I saw them—about 50 Heinkels at somewhere near 18,000 feet, the sinking sun glinting on their light blue under-surfaces. There was a French fighter, a Curtiss, attacking them single-handed, but he didn't seem to be pressing his attacks right home —perhaps cross-fire was getting him bothered. The colonel's wife couldn't see them, but the colonel got quite excited and wanted to see one shot down. We were both disappointed that nothing seemed to happen. He said, " Don't you go up after these bombers? " and I answered, " No, sir, that is for the French Squadrons. We have other work, although we have had to do both jobs up till now." He looked at me rather sharply. Then they bade me *au revoir*, and I watched their red Citroën disappear in the white dust down the road to Paris. I wondered when *we* would see Paris again. . . .

Just about sunset we were all standing in the garden with our noggins, trying to pick out the Hun formations, as we could hear bombing over towards Reims again. We really wanted to sleep more than anything, but, as I have said, these damned paratroops were expected at dusk or dawn, and we naturally wanted to be ready to receive them in the appropriate manner. The visibility was perfect apart from the fluffy white clouds. Suddenly someone pointed, and far, far away to the east we could just pick out a formation of aircraft. We gave a cheer as we saw one give out black smoke and start to go down. It went into a spin, still leaving its trail of smoke, and came down from about 20,000 feet. As it became silhouetted against a towering cumulus cloud, I said, " It looks uncommonly like a Hurricane to me . . . I'm sure it's a Hurricane." The others agreed. We watched, fascinated, as the spinning aircraft crawled slowly down the cloud-mountain, flicking round and round like a leaf falling from a tall tree. We watched for the white blob of a parachute to appear, for the aircraft to come out of its spin, for it to fall in flames, for something quick to happen. But nothing happened. It never came out. And as it dropped and dropped to the base of the cloud, so did our spirits : until finally it disappeared in the evening shadow, leaving nothing but a crooked trail of smoke down the sky to mark its last fight.

" Well," said the Bull suddenly, " I think that deserves a quick drink ! " And we snapped out of it and had one.

* * * * *

At last the red globe of the sun sank below the trees, the stars came out and the light faded, and we could fall on to our camp beds and just go right out. The Bull alone stayed up—I had last seen him bending over the telephone to Wing in the corner of the hall. But it seemed that our heads had scarcely touched our straw pillows when we were woken again. It was midnight. We didn't have to struggle back into full wakefulness as in days gone by, but were wide awake in a flash; or, rather, we were on our feet almost before we realized our whereabouts, automatically buttoning up our tunics and buckling on our revolvers. I don't think we ever really slept now. We'd forgotten what sleep was like, forgotten almost the need of it until we found ourselves falling asleep over an unwanted meal or during a disinterested conversation.

So here we were, back at it again : we were off to Vraux immediately. The air party would proceed to the aerodrome and, if necessary, take the machines off an hour and a half before dawn; anyway they would take off half an hour before dawn. Any aircraft unserviceable to the extent of being temporarily unflyable were to be turned upside down in bomb-craters and burnt. The advance road party, consisting of Knackers' Renault, the buckboard, the Renault van, the Bull's Humber brake, and a Commer van from Wing with Squadron Leader P—— aboard, was to leave now and proceed independently. The main road party, consisting of the remaining Squadron transport, together with all the troops, kit, equipment and petrol-tankers, was to leave absolutely as soon as possible. We didn't know it at the time, but the Huns were already at Rethel, and in the absence of any instructions from H.Q. at Reims the Bull had ordered this move on his own initiative.

His decision was justified by events : the last lorry of the main road party had scarcely crossed the bridge over the Marne-Aisne canal at Berry at 7 a.m. when it was blown up by French sappers; and Moses, the interpreter, who had returned to try and salve some of our Mess equipment, was astonished to see French machine gunners crouching behind cover on the banks of the canal. He was even more astonished when bullets whined overhead and he saw the advance guard of a German Panzer unit coming up the canal. Fortunately the Huns continued along the canal instead of following Moses and the main road party, who were haring down the Reims road, off which they later branched.

For my part, I was detailed to set off straight away in the buckboard. The idea was to disperse the Squadron as much as was feasible so that we should not all suffer the same fate, whatever it might be. As soon as I had got my kit aboard off we cracked—or, rather, that was the idea. But in the darkness it was impossible to do anything but crawl against the dense stream of refugees that was oozing through the village. Occasionally as one passed a couple of carts that had become entangled one heard the excited chatter of arguing voices; but for the most part they moved silently, as if asleep, the only sounds being the creaks from the swaying, rickety carts, the tired cloppety-clop of horses' hooves, the shuffle of weary feet through the dust. It was like a ghost-army re-enacting its last retreat.

We gained the Reims-Laon road and turned down towards Reims. I couldn't see the crucifix, but I knew it was there, and the knowledge somehow was comforting. One often lost sight of God in those days and nights, but one knew He was there, and that was better than food and drink and sleep. The main road wasn't so crowded—most of the refugees were travelling west across it—but quite a lot of cars were passing down it, going much too fast and without any lights. Several times we came to blazing wrecks in the middle of the road. No one knew whether there had been anyone trapped inside, no one stopped to see, no one cared. They must get away—get away—get away from the cursed Boche.

People screamed at us to put our lights out, but we
kept them on. Bombs fell beside the road, but we
kept them on. At last we turned off the main road,
and just as the pale light of dawn began to tinge the
sky we found the aerodrome. We found the wrong
one first, but were re-directed. And as the light
broadened we saw—comforting sight!—the sane,
strong, sturdy British lines of 114 Squadron's
Blenheims glistening in the morning dew.

The Bull soon arrived, then Knackers. The first
consideration was to organize food, and in this
114 Squadron was very helpful. They used a little
café a few miles from the aerodrome as their Mess,
and offered to share it with us. The air party roared
in soon after dawn, which was a relief. We went down
to 114's café, which was beside a canal bridge in a
pleasantly rural setting, and had a very welcome
breakfast. I'm afraid we rather crowded the place
out, but the bomber boys took it all very sportingly
and were most hospitable. As a matter of fact, one
or two of them said they were very glad to have some
fighter boys at hand, for they had been badly strafed
by low-flying Dorniers, and several bombed-up
aircraft had caught fire and been blown to smithereens.
I had seen the remains on the aerodrome.

During breakfast we heard a good many enemy
aircraft about and a lot of bombing : we learnt later
that the Germans were strafing Châlons again—some
of the boys had flown over that morning and said
there was nothing left of it. We were soon back on
the aerodrome, and " B " Flight were sent off. On
their return we were told we wouldn't be needed on
the aerodrome until called, so we had a good lunch
at the café and then lay down on the grass in the shade
of a great chestnut tree and slept. We couldn't sleep
deeply—we were too tired for that. Even the light
breeze continually disturbed us. Eventually I went
over to talk to a friend I had last seen at Penrhos, in
North Wales, in the summer of '38. He had been a
cheerful blond giant then, and many were the tramps

we had had in the Welsh hills, the long swims in the sea, the noggins in the local inn, and the friendly fights in the Mess, smashing tables and chairs and even walls as we crashed and threshed round the room in what we pretended was a death struggle. I was now about to slap him on the back and shake hands, but fortunately someone saw and stopped me. He drew me aside and told me that poor old N—— had been on a low bombing raid with some of the other boys when they had been attacked by Me.109's. N——'s aircraft caught fire, and he was so low that all he could do was to put the thing down as quickly as possible, bombs and all. He had got badly burnt and a bit shaken doing it, but had managed to leap out before the thing went up in flames in earnest. He had returned to try and get his gunner out, but it was no use, and he only got burnt some more. He then ran like hell and threw himself flat just as the bombs exploded. He was shot up on the ground by six 109's, using their cannon, for 20 minutes, but wasn't hit, and managed to get back somehow. And there he was, sitting astride a chair with the back in front of him, trying not to let his eyes betray the pain of his skinless back. I spoke to him a little and tried to cheer him up, but he could hardly answer me, so I left him alone.

The transport didn't arrive till the late afternoon, and when eventually we got down to the village where we were billeted (about a mile from the aerodrome) we had the fag of unloading our camp-beds and hoiking them along to our billets. I was in a pleasant house beside the lovely old church, and I shared what appeared to be the guest, or possibly the bridal, bedroom with Knackers. He won the toss and had the canopied bed, but I didn't really mind where I slept. It was already dark, having just gone eleven, but we could still hear German aircraft about. There was a stationary convoy in the village, which we didn't much like, for we didn't want to be bombed by night as well as by day. The owner of the house was a nice

86

old girl, and showed us with pride her deep cellar, into which, she said, we must all go at the first bomb. We secretly resolved that nothing would get us out of bed that night, bombs least of all. The old girl offered us a drink in the kitchen, and though it was late and we were tired, we had been promised a long rest in bed in the morning, not having to be on the aerodrome till six, so we accepted. The kitchen was warm and cosy, the brass and copper pots and pans glinting dully in the firelight. Did we think the Germans would be here soon? Possibly. Should they leave their home? Not yet. Would we protect them? We would try. Had we shot down many Boches? Yes, but not as many as we were going to shoot down. Were we ever frightened? Yes, often. They didn't understand that one, and we seized the pause it afforded to get up and retire to bed, with many apologies and excuses and good wishes for the night.

We had been in bed scarcely an hour when we were called by a runner and told the whole Squadron was moving again. Bloody hell! We rolled out of bed, pulled on our shoes and coats and tramped along to Johnny's billet. Apparently the Bull had met a column of French tanks rattling through the village that evening going away from the front. The leading tank had stopped just long enough for an excited French captain to stick his head out of the turret and shout to the Bull: "The Boches are already in Reims! They will be here before morning!" They then rattled on again at full speed. This was rather disconcerting, so the Bull rang up H.Q. They didn't seem to know very much about the general position, but said they would ring again at 9 p.m. and give definite instructions. Nine p.m. came, but no call, and when the Bull tried to get on to H.Q. he found the line either broken or cut. He had waited until midnight for communication to be re-established, but it wasn't, so he had ordered this move. He had vowed that, whatever happened and whatever instruc-

87

tions or orders he disobeyed, No. 1 Squadron was not going to be accounted for on the ground. Accordingly he ordered the same procedure as before—advance road party to leave now, main road party and kit when ready, and air party before dawn. This time we were to go to a place called Anglure, some 50 miles to the S.S.W.

I was to go with the air party, and we all went along to the aerodrome to await the approach of dawn. It was cold and damp and desolate, and in our stomachs was that quivering that comes of fatigue and hunger and chilliness.

At about three the 'phone rang. It was Panther (G.H.Q.)—and a very irate Panther, too! Why was the Squadron moving without orders, etc., etc.? Recall them immediately. Well, that was that. Here we were with all our beautiful little aeroplanes and no bloody troops, no bloody equipment, no bloody petrol, no bloody C.O.—in fact, with damn all! Johnny tore his hair. However, one had to make the best of these little things. A message was got through to Anglure, where fortunately 501 Squadron was (they were a reinforcement from England). " B " Flight was left on the aerodrome for aerodrome defence, and we of " A " Flight went off to resume our interrupted sleep. I had great difficulty in getting into my billet—they refused to believe I wasn't a German paratroop—but eventually I was able to fall gratefully into Knackers' bridal bed. We heard later that the tank-captain who had caused all the trouble had been shot.

I slept like a log for three hours and was awakened, greatly refreshed, to go and relieve " B " Flight on the aerodrome. Eventually we got the Squadron together again. The Bull got a raspberry, I believe, but probably he was quite right in the circumstances, and had only anticipated a move that came anyway within 24 hours. The date, by the way, was now the 17th, and the day Friday.

Later that morning " A " Flight was sent off. I

protested to Johnny at not being taken along, but all he said was, " Not this time, Paul. There'll be plenty more." Johnny, Pussy, Killy, Hilly, and S—— were the five. So, disappointed, I had to be content with watching them go off and waiting impatiently for their return; and thinking once again, as I saw them wheel and circle over the aerodrome in formation and climb off to battle, what grand men they were.

After an hour and a quarter we began looking at our watches and wondering what had happened: they should have been back by now. At last we saw the thin line of a Hurricane coming towards us; it came over slowly, gently rocking its wings. They'd had a fight all right. We looked for the letter on the side: " H "—that was Sgt. S——. We watched him park down between the bomb-craters and went over.

He'd certainly had a pasting. As he ran the petrol out of his carburettors we stood by, pointing and laughing at the bullet and cannon-shell holes all over his machine. He was laughing, too, and raised two fingers derisively. " How many? " we asked when he got out. " I got two of the bastards—Me.110's," he answered. " How did they come down? " I asked. " Flamers! " he said, rubbing his hands. " One of them was the sod who did this, too," pointing at his scarred machine. We walked round it counting the holes. There were three cannon-shell holes and about thirty bullet holes: one bullet had entered the fuselage from behind, gone through the slit in the armour-plating behind the pilot's back through which the Sutton harness goes, and had stopped on hitting the harness cable just short of S——'s neck. There were plenty of dents in the armour-plate, too—thank God we had the stuff; it had already saved many lives. S—— did a good job in bringing his machine back, for one of the aileron hinges was severed and all the controls were damaged to some extent. But we had to write the aircraft off on the spot.

Soon all the boys but one came trickling back.

Johnny, Hilly and Killy had each got a 110. Pussy was the missing one. He was missing all the morning. When someone was missing like that we didn't talk of it, didn't even mention his name. It wasn't a conscious effort at tact—we no longer knew the meaning of such a thing—but a natural reticence, a reluctance to discuss possibilities of which everyone was only too well aware. But Pussy turned up all right, as most of us had. He had shot down a 110 and had then been shot down himself in flames, having to bale out. This was his second brolly-hop, his first having been before the Blitz, as already recorded. On this last occasion a couple of French soldiers did target-practice on him as he came down, presumably taking him for a Hun (they always assumed anyone in a parachute automatically to be a Hun), and Pussy was dismayed and discomfited to hear some thirty rifle shots whine past him. However, they all missed, and Pussy was subsequently able to turn his excellent command of the French language to good account.

There was still no news of Leslie and Lorry, and gradually we began to give up hope. We didn't have much time for thinking about them, but they were always in the backs of our minds, and kept coming to the fore when we had a moment to reflect. Lorry, who had come to us from 87 Squadron, was as good a pilot as any of us, and better than some; but he had had consistent bad luck since the Blitz started, and this would make the third time he had been shot down in five days. He already had three Huns to his credit, and had probably increased that score in his last fight. Leslie, on the other hand, had had good luck. He was an Australian, and had thrown himself into the fray with a reckless abandon that was magnificent in its way, having shot down a total of 16 Huns, most of them in the last five days, without once being shot down himself. Presumably he also had increased his score before going down; he was shortly afterwards awarded the D.F.C. We never saw or heard of these

two boys again, and they are now officially presumed
Killed in Action.

* * * * *

Over supper that evening some of us discussed the
German Air Force's tactics and methods. We all
agreed that they didn't seem to like our Hurricanes,
few as they were, for as a sequel to Cobber's story of
the Dornier crew baling out when they saw him, a new
pilot of ours, Peter B——, had sighted a formation of
five Dorniers which had split up and beaten it when
he had appeared all by himself. On the other hand,
the Luftwaffe on the whole was displaying no signs of
cowardice or unwillingness to fight, though usually,
of course, the Germans were in such vastly superior
numbers to us that there would have been little
excuse for that. What we had seen of German
bombing had been extremely effective, partly due to
accuracy, and partly to a ruthless disregard for non-
military "incidentals" surrounding their targets.
We disapproved strongly of the strafing of refugees,
of course, but considered that the individual German
airman was carrying out his orders accurately and
well, as a soldier should, and on the whole fighting
like a gentleman. On the other hand, we hadn't
wanted this bloody war, with all its filthy muck, that
the Germans seemed to think so fine; but we had
been forced to fight. "And now that we are fighting," we thought, "we'll teach you bloody Huns *how*
to fight. We'll shoot your snotty fighters out of the
sky, we'll rip your foul great bombers to shreds, we'll
make you wish to God you'd never seen an aeroplane.
We'll teach you to make war!" We knew we could,
too, *if we were reinforced,* for already our gains had
far exceeded our losses : our Squadron score of enemy
aircraft destroyed for a week's fighting stood at
around the hundred mark for the loss of two of our
pilots missing and one wounded. We knew the Huns
couldn't keep up the pace if we could only have some
numbers to oppose them—and we knew that *we*

91

couldn't keep it up indefinitely without help or relief. But we realized also that there were considerations of "higher strategy" about which we knew nothing, and we trusted our leaders. And so the "strategic withdrawal" continued. . . .

That night the transport and kit left for Anglure. We pilots slept in 114 Squadron's hut on the aerodrome, and took off at six. We had a bit of a job finding Anglure aerodrome, for it turned out to be an undefined collection of fields of different sorts—some full of long grass or vegetables and some just harrowed —dotted with clusters of pine. There was even a wood in the middle of it, and we probably shouldn't have found it at all but for 501 Squadron's Hurricanes parked on it. However, the natural configuration of the ground provided admirable camouflage, which was something.

Nothing much happened that morning beyond a few local patrols. I can't remember whether there were any fights, but at about three that afternoon volunteers were called for to make up a formation of eight to fly to Amiens. A voice inside me said : " Don't be a sap—let some of the fresh boys do it— you'll probably be going home to England in a day or two if you're smart ! " So I stood up and volunteered. Hilly was leading us and would have three with him, and I would follow with another three. Most of those going were pilots who'd joined the Squadron shortly before the Blitz, presumably to enable us to work in reliefs, but we hadn't been able to use them up till now because of their inexperience. Our orders were to go to Amiens, land and refuel, and then do the special job that would be allotted us. We were doubtful whether we could make Amiens in one hop, but we set off.

Everything went smoothly until we reached St. Quentin. Then a lot of light ack-ack opened up on us, and as we were only at 1,000 feet it was pretty hot. We split up at once, turning, diving and climbing individually to present a more difficult target. The

Germans weren't supposed to be within fifty miles, but this stuff was too accurate to be French. It was damned good shooting : black bursts were appearing in clumps of four all over the place, just at the right height and sometimes uncomfortably close, and there was also some smaller stuff that made a sort of ring when it burst, leaving hardly any smoke. Ack-ack bursts always look like spooks to me, suddenly popping out and pulling frightening faces. Anyway, we had scattered and turned to head back when one of the Hurricanes dived down and disappeared. Then I saw three aircraft that I at first took to be Me.110's. I got into position to attack, but they turned out to be Potez 63's, and I saw them dive-bombing. One of them must have been hit by ack-ack for he went down in flames. From all this it was pretty obvious that the Germans, as usual, weren't where they were supposed to be. The French Intelligence reports were regularly twenty-four hours behind.

I was now at about 3,000 feet. The others were forming up on an aircraft in front, but when I went up close I found it wasn't Hilly's " E." It turned out later to be Peter B——, and he was objecting strongly to everyone forming up on him, but couldn't stop them. There were only six of us—Hilly and one other were missing. I had no maps, and hadn't much idea of our whereabouts (it wasn't till afterwards that I learnt the town was St. Quentin); but evidently no one else had either, so I took the lead and started searching for an aerodrome. We saw a town to the south, with a column of grey smoke rising from it to some 4,000 feet and spread out at the top like a giant toadstool. I gave it a wide berth, and after zig-zagging about a bit, we fortunately came to an aerodrome not far from the town where we'd been shot up. A couple of burnt-out Potez 63's lay among some bomb craters on it—and lo and behold, there was a Hurricane taxying in. As I touched down I saw Hilly's " E " on the Hurricane, but was also surprised to see it swing into the wind and take off hastily. I opened my throttle and took off again too; we then formed up and followed back S.E. We learned later that a Frenchman had run up to Hilly on the ground and said, " Get out quick—the Germans are just over there and will be here in five minutes ! " Hilly also had suspected the ack-ack fire of being German. He had seen the Potez's bombing, and his suspicions had been increased by the presence of a Henschel 126 (Hun Army Co-op.) which he had literally blown out of the sky.

We had been in weak mixture for some time, but we were getting very short of petrol when at last we came to Plievaulx, 139 Squadron's aerodrome. There were no aircraft there, but there were some tankers, and we parked down. The tankers were empty, and the troops set-to to refill them from four-gallon cans. We lay down on the grass, and some of us slept.

The C.O. of 139 came over and spoke to us. He said he had lost all his best crews and had just sent his last three Blenheims back to England. When he mentioned his pilots he spoke sadly and looked at the sky. By the time we were finally refuelled it was much too late to go on with the job, and with a feeling akin to relief we at last touched down again in the twilight on our stubble-patch at Anglure. Sgt. A—— was the missing pilot. He was later reported Prisoner of War, so presumably he stopped an unlucky one and had to land.

We got off the aerodrome at 10.30, when it was dark, and went down to get some food at a little café the Bull had found for us in the village. We all crowded in and swallowed some eggs, bread and wine : it might just as well have been sawdust for all our parched tongues could taste of it. I made a nuisance of myself by cross-questioning the boys for my diary notes. No one cared about diaries now—I didn't care myself really, but did it out of force of habit. I sat on after the other boys had left, drinking *fine* that I didn't really want with a French air-gunner, and trying to be bright with the little barmaid, Susette.

She was rather pretty in a coquettish way, but one could scarcely be bothered to look at a woman these days. At midnight I rose and shook hands with the Frenchman, and we wished each other the luck we knew we needed. He was killed the next day.

The village was full of Armée de l'Air, so we had made our encampment under the pine trees in the grounds of a neighbouring château. The moon was waxing, and the château stood gaunt and cold, staring sightlessly at the black woods. My batman had made my bed in the one and only tent, so I had perforce to sleep in it. Most of the boys lay in the soft leaves under the stars.

We knew there was an early start for us in the morning. In the café, *in camera*, we had discussed our latest assignment. Apparently the Huns were not being held. To-morrow the R.A.F. and the Armée de l'Air were sending over all the bombers they could muster to bomb the bridges on the Aisne. The British bombers were being reinforced from the Air Component and from England, and were to be given a cover of three fighter squadrons. But the fighters would not be over the target simultaneously : they would each be over in succession, and for a quarter of an hour apiece. No. 1 Squadron was to be there last, the other two, 73 and 501, first and second. It was emphasized that the success of this bombing raid was vital. We were to be standing by from half an hour before dawn.

I had difficulty in sleeping that night, which was unusual for me. The others seemed to be restless too, tossing and turning and muttering. Perhaps they were only dreaming, as one did, of Messerschmitts and bombs and things; perhaps they were thinking, as I was, of the morning's task. Most likely we were all so damned tired we couldn't relax. However, eventually I sank into dreamland—or rather nightmare land, as it was nowadays.

We were up again at two, groping for our tunics in the dark. We must be just about crawling by now, I thought, for we hadn't taken off more than our sweaty tunics for ten days, and we'd lain ourselves down in all sorts of queer places. We piled into the transport and pushed off to the aerodrome. We knew it was cold because it always was, but we couldn't feel it : only that trembling in the stomach that made us feel weak.

On the aerodrome we lay down round the base of a haystack to await the dawn and the order to take off. We waited, but the order didn't come. It was one of the loveliest dawns I have seen; I lay still in the hay and watched it. By the time the sun had appeared on the horizon the order to take off still hadn't come. We grew restless, and stirred and fidgeted uneasily. This waiting was bad for one; it made one jumpy and even apprehensive. We weren't used to being given our orders to brood on all night, and then by the hour next day : we were used to carrying out an order on the spot and in double-quick time. At last I jumped up and went over to my machine. The Bull's parachute was in it, but he wasn't going on this trip; we were short of packed parachutes for obvious reasons. Incidentally, we had a damned good parachute-packer, thank God—a little Irishman. It had been the custom in peace-time to give our packer 10/- in the unlikely event of our making a jump, and now we gave him 100 francs each time we hopped, so he was waxing rich. I spent an hour pottering about my machine, checking this and that, and altering the parachute-harness to fit me as tightly as possible. I'd learnt the lesson of having a loose harness on my first hop, when I got such a wrench in the groin that I thought I'd stopped a bullet there.

I went back to the hay wishing there was something else to do. I tried to sleep, but couldn't, and kept brooding over our forthcoming trip. I had never felt like this before, and I didn't like it. I thought my nerves and morale must be wearing down. Probably they were, and from previous experience I thought some food might help. I tried to sleep again : no good. I spoke to myself severely and told myself I was a yellow dog. In reply, I admitted I was afraid. I told myself that fear was inadmissible. I answered it was there just the same. " All right," I said to myself, " if that's the unfortunate case, it must be controlled." I knew all this anyway, but still. . . .

I fell to contemplating the quality of courage as it applied to us. I often felt afraid before a job, and though we none of us admitted it, I knew we all felt the same. Once in the cockpit, though, and busied in strapping oneself in and so on, the fear turned to the tension of excitement, which was subjugated in its turn to the concentration required in taking off and joining up in the air. From then on one got no time for thinking of anything but finding the enemy, of searching every visible cubic inch of air, and of seeing him before he saw you. When one did see him, all the tension and concentration of one's body was focussed in a great leap of the heart, a flicking-over in the pit of one's stomach. It always made me swallow a couple of times. After that it was a simple matter : sights switched on, range and wing-span indicators checked, gun-button on " fire," a quick look at the engine-instruments and altimeter, an adjustment on the airscrew-control. Of course, one usually flew with these things ready, and sometimes one got no time for fiddling about; but usually one did. Then, as one went into action, with one's body taut against the straps, teeth clenched, thumb on the gun-button, narrowed eyes intent on getting that black-crossed Hun in the sights and holding him there, one felt one's pumping heart turn to a block of ice. Not in fear. One's brain became coldly clear, and one was in an instant transformed into a cool, calculating killer. You'd think an aerial combat was a hot-blooded, thrilling affair, but it isn't. I've never felt a fighter in a fight—except, perhaps, in the moment of victory, when one feels a savage, primitive exaltation. It's not very nice. . . .

Soon, thank heavens, some breakfast arrived :

97

bread, bully-beef and hot tea. We didn't touch our bully-beef, but we drank that tea in a trice, and then lay back on our hay feeling new men, grateful and refreshed.

All the same, I could see the boys were jumpy. It seems absurd, but I seriously cursed the unfortunate staff officer who had given us our orders, apparently quite unnecessarily, last night. For the next two hours I was continually troubled by something proclaiming itself as a premonition. I got up and walked about kicking things and throwing stones, much to the annoyance of someone who shouted, " For God's sake, Paul, keep still for a moment ! "

At last, at ten o'clock, after seven and a half hours' waiting, the order to take-off came. We walked quickly to our machines. It was the first time I'd seen Johnny looking as he did, or any of the boys for that matter. I threw my tin hat and respirator on the ground beside my aircraft and climbed in. In a few minutes we were formed up; we had not operated against the Huns as a squadron before and were at last able to assess the moral effect of numbers on our own side.

As we climbed up through the 4/10 of cumulus cloud at 12,000 feet, I saw five unescorted Heinkels, in close formation, crossing above and ahead of us from right to left, and called Johnny up to tell him. It broke our hearts to have to leave them alone, but we had to, and that was that. We reached our patrol at 20,000 feet, and spent the time there getting a little extra height. Now and then we caught sight of formations in the distance, but saw none near. Beneath the scattered clouds, at 12,000 feet, there was a slight haze, and we couldn't see our own bombers at all.

After our allotted time was up Johnny turned us for home, and we started diving down gently but quite fast. When we were at about 16,000 feet we suddenly caught sight of a formation of about 25 Blenheims below us and going the same way. They

22   BRITISH BOMBS ON AN ENEMY CONVOY

23   MORE BRITISH BOMBS ON AN ENEMY-HELD AERODROME

were just below the cloud-level, and we cheered to ourselves to see them. Someone called up, " Good show—there they go ! " Yes, it *was* a good show : it was nice to see some British bombers for a change. They looked strong and deadly and brave in their compact formation. We came down behind them in a series of S-turns in quite close formation, smiling to ourselves : it was a good sight. We meant to escort them back to their bases, or, at any rate, as far as we could.

As we came down nearer, however, and examined them more closely as they slid along steadily in and out of the small clouds, we began to think there was something fishy about those Blenheims. Suddenly Johnny ordered : "Echelon starboard—echelon starboard—go. They're bloody Heinkels ! " We could see the black crosses now on their dull-grey wings. I was No. 3 in " A " Flight, i.e., on Johnny's left, and slid underneath him to come up on Hilly's right in Echelon Starboard. This was the first formation attack we'd had a chance of making, and the first unescorted bombers we'd come across, too. One squadron of Hurricanes *versus* 25 Heinkels—nice work ! Now perhaps we'd be able to give back to the bombers something of what they'd made us feel from time to time !

We went in astern of them in good formation, Johnny taking the left-hand aircraft of the enemy formation, Hilly taking the second, and myself the third, leaving Yellow section of " A " Flight to come up on our right. We'd practised this attack dozens of times in peace-time, and it almost seemed like a practice now, except that the Hun rear-gunners were shooting. The Huns had closed up their formation into sub-formations of threes in Vic, some having a fourth " in the box " (i.e., below and behind the leader of a three). The sub-formations were stepped down and spread out from the front, which consisted of one Vic of three, and each sub-formation appeared to be covering another one with its fire. Their formation was good, and they appeared to be an efficient squadron (you must realize that all that one sees and does in an air-action takes only a few seconds).

As we went in, closing the range and holding our fire, we could see the smoke of the Huns' tracer-bullets snaking through the air towards us. Remorselessly closing in, I was tempted almost to feel sorry for the Hun bombers—but evidently they weren't feeling sorry for us, for the fire suddenly got hotter. I was coming up behind the left-hand aircraft of a sub-formation of four when I noticed with considerable uneasiness that I seemed to be the focal point of a lot of tracer-lines. At that point I betrayed bad discipline, if good sense, by swerving across to a position astern of the right-hand aircraft of the sub-formation. Just then Sgt. S—— called up, " Look out behind —behind you ! "—and before we had even fired a shot we broke up, thinking fighters were attacking us from the rear. (It was ascertained afterwards that a Hurricane got in S——'s sights as he was about to fire, and I rather think it must have been me.) That spoiled our nice little formation attack, and the flight recommenced on a basis of individual attacks—all the more unfortunate because this German formation seemed to have " fire-control," i.e., a " fire-controller " in one of the aircraft (usually the leader's) tells all the rear-gunners which enemy aircraft to fire at, so that they can concentrate simultaneously upon one. Obviously the best counter to fire-control is a simultaneous attack by as many fighters as possible, and this is most conveniently done in formation.

I had pulled away above and to the right of the Huns, in a position I judged to be out of their effective range. As I decided which one to go for, I saw two or three drop down with Hurricanes firing astern of them, two with their engines smoking and a third with its wheels down as well. I then dived down to the left and turned right again to come up astern of a Hun who had dropped back a bit in the middle of the formation. I was closing, and just about to open fire, when I heard Hilly's voice shouting, "Behind you—behind you—look out for God's sake!" I pulled up to the right again to have a look, seeing another Hurricane pulling away to the left. Then I saw what Hilly had been shouting about—thank God he did! A Heinkel that had been damaged and dropped astern had somehow managed to pull himself together again and had been coming along flat-out behind me; he would probably have got me but for Hilly's warning. I heard Hilly say, "The bastard!" and saw a Hurricane I took to be his attack the Heinkel, which I think went down. I thought the Hun had put up rather a good show and was sorry in a way to see him go. But thanks, Hilly!

I now tried again. I went in astern of the extreme right-hand aircraft of a rear sub-formation of three. I had fired several bursts and was converging fast when I got in his slipstream and my sights came off. I was nearly on top of him, and judging by the way he suddenly slowed down I think his engines must have been damaged. I pulled out quickly to the left and then turned in on him again, steeply banked to the right, to fire a good burst into his front cockpit, allowing deflection. I pulled away to his right and saw him do a sort of cartwheel, quarter-rolling to the right and dropping his nose simultaneously to the vertical. He went straight into a vertical spiral, and though I saw no smoke or flames, I think he was a gonner, for big bombers don't do things like that for fun. Probably the pilot was dead or otherwise unserviceable; anyway, he was out of the formation, which was the main thing.

I now took a quick look round and saw only one Hurricane still present. I'd been rather long-winded, and presumed that most of "A" Flight had finished their ammunition and gone home. I still had plenty left, and went in astern of another Heinkel on the left of the formation. Just as I was closing, a whole clump of ack-ack bursts broke out in the rear of the formation, extending all around me. I glanced across to the left and saw the other Hurricane similarly surrounded with bursts, but going straight on. A shell must have burst just beneath me, for I heard a muffled bang and saw a lot of bits come up through my port wing. The aircraft gave a sort of jerk, like hitting a bump, but I wasn't going to lose that damned lagging Heinkel, and kept straight after him. He was going flat-out to catch up, and he'd nearly done so when I had him in range and opened fire.

Between bursts I noticed I was getting a hell of a lot of cross-fire from the formation, and heard several pops and saw a lot of holes appear in both wings. I was more surprised when there was a bang, and a cannon-shell opened a big hole in my port wing. Tough, those boys! But I was surprised how calm I felt, and how coolly I was thinking. I remember making a mental note of that rear-cannon, and that those Heinkels were Mark V's. Suddenly smoke poured from both my Heinkel's engines, his wheels dropped, and he went down in a shallow diving turn to the right. I let him go and pulled up to the left.

I still had about 100 rounds or more to each gun left, I judged, and I was delighted to see a Heinkel swerve and break formation as a clump of ack-ack shells burst in his sub-formation of three. He dropped behind and below, but immediately regained control and opened up flat-out to catch up again. Nevertheless, he'd lost some two hundred yards or so, and naturally I pounced on him, going in astern and opening fire almost straight away. I saw another sub-formation of three, with one in the box, ahead, above and to the right, and they were firing at me for all they were worth. I concentrated on my Heinkel again. I had him beautifully steady in the sights, and poured short savage bursts into him as I closed. I was wondering why he showed no signs of being hit, because I knew I was hitting him, and he had nearly caught up, when suddenly grey smoke streamed from both his engines, then from his wing-roots and fuse-lage, and in a second he was completely enveloped in

24   THE MOMENT OF VICTORY : A HEINKEL 111 ABOUT TO GO IN

25   AND AFTERWARDS : THE END OF A HEINKEL IN A FRENCH FIELD

26   BACK ON THE JOB, 1941

it. I felt that savage thrill again, and said, " And that for luck, you sod ! " as I fired a final burst into the burning mass. It was only half a burst, because I ran out of ammunition with a hiss of escaping compressed-air. As I broke away in leisurely fashion to the left, feeling pretty pleased with myself, I glanced at the still-firing sub-formation up to the right and mentally put two fingers up. It was then that I learnt a lesson I should have known, and will never forget.

Just as I rolled over to the left to dive away I saw the sudden flash of tracer very near me, and in the same second there were several pops and then a loud " Bang ! " in my right ear. (I think it came from the boys up to the right, but it's just possible that the rear-gunner of the burning Heinkel was still firing, and if so I take my hat off to him.) Anyway, in that instant I knew they'd hit my aeroplane. Almost at once there was a shower of blood down my right side. The aircraft was diving almost vertically, and with surprise I saw my right arm, drenched in blood, bent up in front of me against the hood. There was no feeling in it, and the hand was bent over like a dead bird's claw. All this happened in a flash ; but so quickly does the mind work that, in the same moment, I guessed at and assessed the damage, and decided what I must do. That " Bang ! " was still ringing in my right ear, and I said to myself straight off : " Can-non shell in right shoulder—arm probably almost severed—write off that arm for good—pull out of dive with left hand and if necessary bale out, pulling rip-cord with left hand."

To my horror, however, I found my left arm wouldn't move either ! I looked down to see where it was, and saw it straight down by my side. I looked up again to find the aircraft plunging earthwards, out of control ; it was going down in a series of dives and swoops, interspersed with momentary flattening-out. Inside the cockpit I had the extraordinary sen-sation of my head being isolated from the rest of my body. I was perfectly conscious, and could hear the rushing hiss of the wind over the cockpit roof. I could see my body before me, and tried with all my strength to move my arms. My right hand, still clawed, was within four inches of the hood-handle, but try as I might I couldn't get it any nearer. The ground was rushing up; I could hear myself gasping and straining to move. And then suddenly I heard myself start to scream. Muffled but clearly audible, I heard myself say it, then shout it, then scream it : "God! God! I'm going to be killed! God!" Then I stopped screaming and looked into the bottom of the cockpit, thinking, "I won't feel it." Then I looked up again and saw the ground still coming up, and nearer—and suddenly my left arm recovered. So obsessed had I become with the idea of getting out that my hand flew immediately to the hood-handle to pull it back. But it was stuck! Jammed! I heaved frantically with all the strength of desperation, but it didn't yield an inch. I looked again, thinking of fire. And then my right hand suddenly flopped down on to the stick, I pulled it back, and out of that hellish dive I came. None too soon either, though not desperately low—at about 2,000 feet, to be exact.

I said to myself, "My God! That's the narrowest squeak I ever want! Now you get down as quickly as possible—you may be on fire or anything, and your engine's stopped anyway." I glanced over the instruments and noticed my air-speed indicator wasn't registering at all—probably a bullet, or that shell, had got the Pitot or some other part of the system. There were lots of holes in the wings, and a bullet hole in the windscreen just to the right of the bullet-proof part. I wondered where the bullet had gone. I was beginning to feel pain now in the right side of my neck and face, and thought a cannon-shell had struck the side of the cockpit and blown a chunk out of me. I still couldn't get the hood open. I circled as I glided down, picked a field near a village so that I could get help quickly, pumped my flaps down, and went in to land with my wheels up. As I held off over a harrowed field I braced myself with my left hand against the sight-bar. I touched, and then bumped and bucketed along the ground, grinding across the field in a cloud of dust. I remember blood splashing forward over the dashboard and wind-screen. Then, just as I thought we were going over, the tail came down with a bump and we came to rest.

Immediately I pulled the pin out of my Sutton harness, undid my parachute, and tried again to open the hood. It was still stuck firm, so I put both feet against the instrument panel and tugged. No: it wouldn't move. I was beginning to feel more pain now in my neck and shoulder, and was feeling rather weak, so I rested a moment. From the bottom of the cockpit little wisps of smoke or dust—I wasn't sure which—were rising. I seized the hood-handles once more, and heaved and strained with all my strength, but the thing didn't budge an inch, and I had to rest again. This was bloody: it looked as though I had escaped a comparatively pleasant death by diving into the ground only to be burnt alive now. I wondered if the first flash of flame would give me the strength to break out of this damned cockpit, or, if not, whether death would come quickly in the heat and smoke. Once again I doubled my efforts, but it was no good. The emergency-panel on the right will not come out with the hood closed, but with my fist I biffed out the small break-out panel in the left side of the hood, and put my arm through it, for no reason other than to have just some access to the outside.

Why the hell didn't those bloody Frenchmen get a move on? I could hear something dripping and smelt petrol. This made me pull myself together for a final effort—and suddenly, with a jerk, the hood came half open. I hauled myself out on to the star-board wing and ran away from the machine in case it blew up. I was panting and exhausted, and stumbled about thirty yards towards a wooded stream. Then

I stopped and looked back. There was no sign of smoke or fire. I went slowly back. I noticed some things, such as the quietness and the heat, very clearly; others, such as the holes I had previously seen in my aircraft, not at all. Presumably a bullet, or perhaps a shell, had damaged the hood-runners, but I forgot to look. I stood on the wing and leant into the cockpit, switching off the reflector sight, turning off the petrol and main engine switches, putting the gun-button to " safe," and taking out my maps, all in a methodical and automatic way. I walked round to the other side, carrying my helmet and maps. I was getting a good deal of pain now, and kicked in the panel where the first-aid kit was kept to get some morphia; but it was a new aeroplane, and there was no first-aid. I swore, and then told myself not to be a sissy and that I only had a bit of a scratch on the neck anyway. All the same it hurt. I didn't know it at the time, of course, but an armour-piercing bullet had struck me on the side of the neck, nicking the angle of the jaw in entering, exposing the jugular vein, and lodging against the spine at the base of the neck. It was the shock against the spine that had caused the temporary paralysis. A little harder, and the paralysis would have been permanent—i.e., until I hit the ground. A little to one side—a fraction of a millimetre would have been enough—and I would have bled to death within five minutes. A little less height, and I would have dived in. A little bit of fire, or an uncontrollable aircraft, and I couldn't even have baled out. A little more or a little less of this or that—but what the hell? I was just lucky.

At last two French soldiers hailed me a couple of fields away, aiming their rifles at me. I put up my hands, but was too weak to keep them right up, and they fell to my shoulders. The Frenchmen, who had started to advance slowly, immediately stopped and took aim again. I put them up once more, but couldn't make it and eventually fell down, panting and with everything swimming. I got up again, and mercifully two cars suddenly arrived with a rush and out jumped a French officer and some soldiers.

They all ran towards me, pointing their revolvers, and seeing their small new-type helmets, I thought for a moment that they were Germans and that I was done for. They quickly surrounded me, and I said, " I'm English—look at the markings on my aeroplane." The officer said, " Oh, mon pauvre ! " and helped me towards the car. He said he had seen me coming down, and had also seen me shoot down the Hun just before. " There he is," he said, pointing to a column of smoke rising behind a wood. I said I had got two others as far as I could tell, and he immediately broadcast the news, and everyone looked at me as if I were some sort of superman. I certainly felt anything but at the time, and felt even worse when a bearded poilu, much to the officer's annoyance, took a good look at where I presumed my wound to be, and said in horrified tones and with staring eyes: " O mon Dieu, il a tout le côté ouvert ! "

Well, to hurry the tale along, we drove at breakneck speed to a French hospital at La Ferté-sous-Jouarre (not far from Château-Thierry), where I was briefly examined, had a bandage slapped on and a shot of anti-tetanine in the leg, and was then shoved into an ancient ambulance on a stretcher, and sent off to another hospital 80 kilometres west, as this one was evacuating. They wouldn't give me morphia for some reason, so I just had to lie hanging on to a rail with my left hand and stick it for four or five hours while the ambulance jolted and lurched along. " Il a l'air de souffrir . . ." said one of the nursing orderlies, very truly. " Il est shocqué," said the other one, which was fortunately also true. I suppose I have had no greater pain in my life, though doubtless others have. I felt that it could be no worse, and that if it was I couldn't stick it. But I knew I *could* stick it as it was, because there was no alternative.

Eventually, after bumping along several country lanes, reversing into fields, and so on, the driver confessed he couldn't find the hospital, and so I managed to persuade him to take me to the American Hospital in Paris, which was only 25 kilometres away. As each sentry challenged us the driver called "aviateur anglais—il a déscendu trois Boches!"—and he said the same to each policeman or bystander as he asked the way. At last we arrived at the American Hospital at Neuilly, and the driver jumped down with his "aviateur anglais—il a déscendu trois!" again, and asked if I could be admitted. I heard a woman's voice, speaking French with a slight American accent, say, "Ils ont du courage, vous savez!" I smiled, as one does at the layman's views on flying, but found a certain warm comfort in her words.

I tried to get up and walk into the hospital, for I felt damned silly lying down like that, but I was pressed back gently, and relaxed not ungratefully. As I was carried through the door out of the bright sunlight into the cool darkness inside, a pretty woman with blonde hair, in the uniform of the American Ambulance Corps, pressed my hand, in which I still clutched my blood-stained flying helmet, and said, "It's going to be all right!" She spoke in English with an American drawl, and I thought at the time that she had the sweetest voice I had ever heard and looked more beautiful than anyone I had ever seen. I felt my eyes fill with sudden tears, and all I could do was to nod and smile my gratitude.

Soon Doc R——, who with several others of the staff had been a great friend of the Squadron at Etretat at the beginning of the war, came to see me. I got him to ring up the Embassy to tell them to let the Squadron know I was O.K. Actually for some reason the message got no further than B.A.F.F. H.Q. at Coulommiers, and Hilly spent two whole days searching French hospitals for me. Doctor de Martell, the celebrated head-specialist, took the bullet out of me two hours later—at about six o'clock. Sally, a young American nurse, very kindly held my hand until I went under. For thirty hours after coming round I vomited at intervals of about half an hour—a most painful proceeding. Not having had a drink since eight o'clock on the morning of the fight, I felt hellish thirsty, but I couldn't take anything. I suppose I was more or less semi-conscious; the vision of that dive kept recurring to me, and I would hear again and again my voice shouting, " God ! I'm going to be killed ! " This would promptly make me vomit once more. It wasn't at all pleasant.

However, with the excellent attention I received, I made a rapid recovery. My operation was on Sunday, May 19th. On Sunday, May 26th, I was more or less sitting up, bearded and sore, but happy, when who should come in but Lew and S——, the latter with a well-deserved Flight-Sergeant's crown on his sleeve. Soon Johnny, Boy, Prosser, Stratters and Killy turned up too. They were on their way home to England, having been relieved, and were in terrific spirits.

Johnny said : " Well, you silly old sod, how the hell did you manage this? Good show, anyway." He told me that the fight on the 19th had been their last of any note. S—— said he had shot down a couple when one of his wing-tanks had stopped an incendiary and caught fire. He then dived so fast that he blew the fire out, subsequently forced-landing successfully near Château-Thierry. He went into the nearest town on foot to get transport, but no one was of much help or even interested. Shortly afterwards the Germans gave the town a pretty thorough bombing, and S—— saw a lot of French soldiers in a panic throwing women and children out of air-raid shelters so that they could get in themselves. He then saw the said women and children blown to bits, arms and legs and miscellaneous bits of flesh flying all over the place. To round things off, the hospital was destroyed by dive-bombers. Johnny said we only got about eight of the Heinkels in our fight, which wasn't much good. He added that he and the boys were going back to England to form a Fighter School under the

Bull, who had already gone, and that they hoped that they would be in time to give the as yet untried English squadrons some tips, and put the experience we had gained at their disposal before the Germans attacked the British Isles. He concluded by telling me that it was fixed for me to go and join them when I was fit; but in my heart of hearts I still cherished notions of rejoining the re-formed Squadron. Had I known it, I was not to be able to fly again for six months, and not to fight again for a further five.

After they had gone I fell to thinking over the events of the past months. Those of the last few days, of course, made previous happenings seem unreal, and even largely obliterated them. Those nine days of hard fighting, from May 10th to May 19th, themselves seemed dream-like now. Lying there in quietness between cool white sheets, my once sweaty and verminous uniform again clean and draped on a chair, I had only the hole in my neck to remind me that they had really happened. On the other hand, the Squadron record was concrete enough, and I had made notes of it :

> *From landing in France on September 9th,* 1939, *until May 9th,* 1940 : 26 enemy aircraft destroyed, our losses 1 new pilot.
> *From May 10th,* 1940, *until May 19th* : 114 enemy aircraft (mostly fighters) destroyed; our losses 2 pilots missing, 2 wounded, and 1 prisoner of war.

Total : 140 enemy aircraft destroyed.

Considering our casualties, this is a record that will probably never be equalled. The figures may seem almost incredible, but in spite of the difficulty of confirming victories, they are not exaggerated. The Squadron's policy was to underclaim, and it was often found that we had shot down more in a combat than we asked credit for. A very careful record of victories was kept in the Squadron. Unfortunately it is possible that it was not credited with its full share, for just before the Blitz our Intelligence Officer had had a breakdown and was sent away, and we didn't get a replacement until much later. As a result, Knackers, who was busy on other work, had to try to make up combat reports in his spare time (if any) in the evenings, and send them in to H.Q. Very often he didn't get time, or couldn't get hold of the pilots. All the same, an accurate log was kept in the Squadron itself, as I have said—but in point of fact none of us gave a damn about scores anyway. All we cared about was that we'd made a slight dent in the Luftwaffe—even though it *was* rather like throwing stones into the oncoming surf—and that we could at least claim victory for the Squadron as a whole.

Our success, I think, was due to a combination of elements: *one*, our Commanding Officer's grasp of essentials, his shrewdness and foresight, and his personal initiative; *two*, the leadership of our two Flight Commanders, Johnny and Prosser; *three*, our peacetime training, which stressed the importance of teamwork; *four*, our gradually acquired war experience; *five* (last but not least), our Hurricanes. It may be of interest to note here that the original members of No. 1 Squadron were decorated for their work in France to the tune of ten Distinguished Flying Crosses (the Bull, Johnny, Prosser, Hilly, Pussy, Leslie, Killy, Stratters, Boy, and myself), and three Distinguished Flying Medals (Sergeants S——, B——, and C——).

*   *   *   *   *

Soon I was moved into a room with a French Captain, who was blind. He was a nice little man and we got on well. We used to listen a lot to the " Bulletins d'Information " on his wireless. Things weren't looking too bright, but as the Frenchman said, " . . . on se débrouillera." Doc R—— came in to see us when he got time. He thought the news depressing, too; the German push from Sedan, having swept through the Champagne district, had turned away from Paris north-west, and was making for the Channel ports. Everyone said that Paris was very well defended—" and I have great faith in the French Army," said Doc R——, voicing our feelings in the matter.

Incidentally, a lot of wounded were arriving now from that same army. They were nearly all head cases (for Dr. de Martell), mostly shell-splinters. Several of the poor devils were insane, and their shrieks and moans could be heard echoing down the long corridors; I have never heard such a blood-curdling or utterly hopeless sound. But Doc R—— said it was surprising how many eventually recovered —80 per cent., I think he estimated. There was only one airman in the place besides myself—a Frenchman who was severely burnt—and no other British wounded.

After a fortnight I insisted on getting up, and was allowed to do so. I had lost over a stone and felt very silly and weak, but I wanted to regain my strength as quickly as possible. I couldn't turn my neck, of course, and a muscle in my right shoulder wasn't working, because the nerve had been largely destroyed. However, it was fun to be about again, and I spent many hours pottering in the garden or on the roof. Once I watched de Martell operating on a man's head. A piece of skull about 4 inches by 4 had been removed, and as de Martell probed and delicately cut the brain with his marvellously steady hands, at last producing the shell-splinter with a " Look now, Monsieur—look well now! "—I was surprised to feel suddenly sick and to have to go outside. Doc R—— came with me, laughing. He said: " I'm glad to see that. I don't feel so bad now." I asked him what he meant, and he replied : " Well, we couldn't face some of the things you do up there, like diving at four or five hundred miles an hour, and it makes me feel better to find that you boys can't face down here what we can."

I often wanted to express my admiration for the work of this hospital staff. They were mostly Americans, with a couple of French doctors and several Swiss, Dutch, Danish, Swedish, English and

French nurses. Now that the wounded were coming in, de Martell and R—— worked day after day continuously from seven in the morning until four the following one. The other doctors were just as indefatigable, and the nurses never lacked in courage, energy or cheerfulness. I thought they were all magnificent, and I shall never forget their kindness to me.

* * * * *

On June 3rd, just before lunch, the Paris sirens wailed. I was having a chat with Doc R—— downstairs, and hearing ack-ack, he and I took the lift to the roof. The firing was heavy, and we could hear the dull droning in the sky of many aeroplanes. "Well, here it is," said R——, as we stood beneath a small roof to avoid shell-fragments. There was a hell of a row going on—bangs and crumps and whistles and the clatter of bits. I stepped out and stared up through the heat-haze : I could hear them all right, but I only saw, between the fluffy clouds, two bombers and the flash in the sun of an escorting fighter. Great billows of black and grey smoke were rolling across the city, from St. Denis, the Seine, and St. Germain to the west. In about twenty minutes the last of the bombers had droned away, to the accompaniment of the faint rattle of machine-gun fire from French fighters. We looked at the smoke and dust-laden air, and then at each other, and grinned a bit sheepishly.

"I'm glad we painted out our red crosses, anyway," remarked Doc R——, as we went down to lunch.

"Berlin to-night . . ." I said. I was right.

* * * * *

Perhaps I had got up and gone about too soon, for I suddenly developed a temperature and went back to bed for a day or two, feeling bloody. More and more wounded were rolling in, the hospital was practically full, and the whole staff was working to capacity. Several of the women ambulance drivers had reported being shot up by Hun aircraft, and one drove back very pluckily with a bullet in her buttock. Several ambulances had disappeared without trace and were presumed to have become casualties. The Huns were without doubt deliberately strafing vehicles marked with the red cross, and the hospital authorities ordered all insignia to be removed.

A French tank captain was brought in. His tank had knocked out four German ones before finishing up locked head-on with a fifth, both of them catching fire. He said the French tanks were superior to the German, but of course heavily outnumbered. He also said the Huns were spread-eagling their prisoners on the fronts of their tanks and using them as rams or collision-mats, though I can't vouch for the truth of that. A French doctor said that he had attended many German prisoners, and considered their extraordinarily excited condition could only be attributed to the use of drugs. This applied particularly to the airmen, he said. I discounted his words at the time, knowing the unbalancing effect of strain in aerial fighting, and especially of being shot down. But if he was right, would it explain the Germans' fatalistic method of mass attack, seen both in the air and on the ground? Would it explain that split-second superiority in reaction that we ourselves had invariably found we had over the Huns in combat?

On June 5th I asked permission to become an out-patient to free a much-needed bed. A friend of mine in the American Embassy, Walter W——, very kindly let me stay at his flat, and the next few days I spent, unwisely but happily, bathing and lying in the sun at the Racing Club in the Bois, teetering about from café to restaurant, from restaurant to bar, eating, drinking, and spending too much, but rejoicing in, and never so grateful for, being alive. Paris as a whole retained its irresponsible gaiety—though one felt it was even rather too irresponsible. The couples still sipped their champagne and sang the choruses of romantic songs in the boulevard cafés. Albert still bowed one in with a portly gesture and a welcoming smile at Maxim's. The Ritz Bar was still in full swing before lunch and again before dinner. The only thing changed was the almost total absence of soldiers.

It was as I walked down the Champs Élysées towards the Concorde one afternoon that I came upon Cobber, of 73 Squadron, sitting at a pavement table with the 73 Squadron Doctor and a well-known journalist. Over a drink Cobber told me that the rest of the original 73 had gone back to England, and that they had been re-formed, like us. He had stayed behind to help get things going, but was off in a couple of days' time. He was on a few hours' leave now. He said they'd had some losses—about five killed, I think—and in answer to my question told me his own personal score of Huns was 17. I noticed, but without surprise in the circumstances, that he seemed nervous and pre-occupied, and kept breaking matches savagely in one hand while he glowered into the middle distance. Like the rest of us, he'd had enough for a bit.

The following day a Hurricane roared down and beat up 73's aerodrome south-west of Paris. To finish up with it did a couple of flick-rolls in succession at 200 feet, and foolishly attempted a third with insufficient speed. Naturally it spun off. It straightened out promptly enough, but of course had no height and went in. The rescue squad was shocked to find an identity disc marked with Cobber's name on the body. So died Cobber.

*   *   *   *   *

On the evening of the day of the Paris raid I had gone along to the A.P.N.A. (the professional aviators' club) in the Avenue Kléber. Usually it was an extremely cheerful place, but that night there was an intolerable air of gloom about it. I had arrived in high spirits and looking forward to having a drink with " Fifi " F—— (a well-known test-pilot), M—— (a captain in the French Air Force), and R—— (one of the Armée de l'Air's leading test-pilots), who were all friends of mine. But Fifi was the only one there. He was very dismal, and told me that M—— had been killed in combat with the German bombers over Paris that morning, and that R—— was *au front* with a fighter squadron. I went off to bed shortly afterwards, having caught the general depression.

Fifi and I met several times for drinks thereafter, and on Sunday, June 9th, he asked me to lunch at the " Popôte des Ailes," the French test-pilots' Mess at Villacoublay. We drove out in his little Simca (Baby Fiat) and found a crowd waiting for us in the bar of the café that contained their Mess. All the well-known professional pilots were there, and many others whose names I forget, though I have their signatures on a menu. Having thrown dice to see who would pay for the food, and again for the wine—a daily custom, I learnt—we trooped across a small garden into the mess-room. It was hung with the prop off an early Morane, the fin off something else that had killed its pilot, and so on. The walls were covered with signed photographs of the past and present members of the Mess, which included every well-known pilot France had had. They showed me round, pointing out the various people : " *He* was lost in the Atlantic; *he* was killed in Syria; *this one's* aeroplane broke in the air; *his* motor cut and he spun in at Buc. . . ." Most of them were dead. There was a certain romance about these professional pilots, many of them with burns or broken bones from former crashes, with sombre eyes, but all gay, reckless and courageous —what we in the R.A.F. call " regardless "—as only French pilots can be.

Fifi bought the food; C——, a pilot with whom I was shot-up over Arras in October, 1939, bought the wine; and " Memère," the fat old girl who had run this café for " her " pilots for over 20 years, and only charged them when she knew they could afford it, served the lot. After lunch they sang a drinking song to me—an adaptation, for Hitler's benefit, of a song once sung by the French sailors about Queen Anne of England. The proceedings came to an abrupt conclusion when news came in of a crash at Villacoublay, and everyone departed hurriedly, leaving Fifi to return me to Paris.

I felt at the time that there was a certain air of finality about that lunch, and that the shadow of the German Army was already spreading over Paris, so that I wasn't entirely surprised now to see a lot of Parisians " on the move," with baggage strapped to their cars and mattresses on the roofs. The Germans seemed to be making for the capital now, coming up the Seine from Rouen. In fact, they were already uncomfortably near, and I felt I couldn't risk staying any longer. Had I known at the time how little stood in the path of the German Army I should have been gone long before.

Accordingly, on Monday, June 10th, I packed my kit, said " Good-bye and thank you " to the American Hospital, and got an " Ordre de Mission " from the R.A.F. Assistant Provost Marshal to travel by train to Blois. The Embassy had left, and I was only able to find out where Panther (H.Q., A.A.S.F.) was from a friend of mine of the Columbia Broadcasting System. On my way to the Gare de Lyon in an Air Force lorry (there were no taxis left) I bought a hat for my wife. We couldn't get near the station, for it was surrounded to a depth of about half a mile by a dense crowd of people trying to get in. We tried the Austerlitz, to find it much the same, but succeeded in ploughing our way through to a platform where we found a harassed official. He said the lines were continually bombed, that there was no time-table, and that the trains were crammed anyway. So with regret I returned and told the A.P.M. he would have to take me with him somehow in the morning. Naturally he wasn't too pleased, for he was full up already; and besides, he'd have to make a *détour* to drop me at Blois, for he was making for Nantes by small by-roads to avoid the traffic. However, he told me to be ready at his H.Q. at five in the morning.

That evening I spent wandering about the city in a rather aimless fashion. The shops and restaurants were boarded up, the streets were deserted except for an occasional heavily laden car, and an air of gloom and desolation had settled over the place. After it was dark I walked up the Champs Elysées to the Étoile, and stood for some time beneath the Arc de Triomphe looking at the tomb of the Soldat Inconnu. The light of the Flamme flickered fitfully up Napoleon's great arches, and over the inscription on the stone slab below : " Ici repose un soldat français, mort pour la patrie." A cloaked gendarme appeared from out of the gloom and stood beside me. He didn't say anything ; I expect we were thinking much the same things.

At 5 a.m. on Tuesday, June 11th, we assembled outside the A.P.M.'s H.Q. It was light, but there seemed to be a fog over the city. There was also a peculiar burning smell, and it wasn't hard to guess that something was on fire somewhere. In the distance we could hear the continuous shaking rumble of heavy gunfire : hell must be popping out there. Soon we were all ready except for one man. We wasted two and a half hours looking for the damned fellow before we found him, but at last we moved off. Our little convoy consisted of the A.P.M.'s car, a lorry carrying 15 R.A.F. Service Policemen and our baggage, and two outriders in the form of despatch-riders on motor-bikes, who proved invaluable in getting us along.

Soon we were in the open country, but the roads were crammed with cars driving three and four abreast, not to mention carts, push-bikes and even perambulators. I looked through the rear window for a last time at the deserted city, with its shroudlike pall of smoke hanging over it. That smoke persisted for some 40 miles. We learnt later that it came from immense quantities of oil fired by the French down the Seine. It blackened all our faces, and made our two despatch-riders look like a couple of niggers. They

118

were damned good riders, and worked unceasingly at straightening out traffic jams, shepherding our little convoy along, and generally introducing an air of calm efficiency where there had previously existed only a jabbering muddle of gradually rising panic.

At last we arrived at Châteaudun, in the castle of which were stored many treasures from the Louvre. We had heard a Royal Air Force Squadron was stationed there, and intended getting some petrol from them, but we couldn't find the aerodrome, and so proceeded down the road towards Blois. Had I only known it, my old Squadron, No 1, was the one stationed at Châteaudun. However, we soon came to an aerodrome on the right of the road with some Battles parked on it, and were directed to a small village on the left where we found 103 Squadron installed. W/Cmdr. D——, their C.O., made us welcome and gave us lunch. Learning my old Squadron was up the road I decided to drop off there. I had my kit, complete with my wife's hat, dumped off, and said good-bye to the A.P.M. with many thanks.

Poor D—— was very " bloody minded," for he had lost nearly all his pilots—almost entirely through having to carry out tasks left undone by the French Army, such as the destruction of bridges. Our old friends of 12 Squadron had lost 24 complete aircrews— i.e., 72 flying personnel—and only six of the original squadron pilots were left. These Battle and Blenheim boys of the A.A.S.F. were the real heroes. We fighter boys at least had a pretty deadly aeroplane in our hands, and had the consolation of chalking up a score. But the bomber boys had little of the thrill, little of the " glamour," so to speak, and twice the danger. They knew that, under the then existing conditions, every time they took the air they didn't stand much chance of returning; but they never shirked a job and never hesitated. I think we all took our hats off to those boys, and it was our greatest sorrow that we were physically unable to give them the protection planned for them.

When I rejoined my re-formed squadron I found

that Squadron Leader P——, from Wing, was in command, and that Hilly was one of the Flight Commanders. Sgt. C—— was still there, as was Knackers, as irrepressible as ever, keeping up everyone's spirits as he invariably had done throughout the French campaign. That evening three mysterious civilians arrived at the château the Squadron was using to collect all the secret documents, which they did after P—— had checked them up by telephone with H.Q. The rumour was that the French were going to pack their hand in, and that the Squadron was to go to Corsica. All non-essential documents were destroyed, and all the kit was packed ready to move at a moment's notice.

Actually the French did hang on a bit longer (in Eastern France they went on fighting for some time after the Armistice), and the Squadron didn't leave for England until June 18th, having operated from several different aerodromes and advance landing-grounds, and covered the British embarkation at Nantes. They added a further 15 Huns to our original score (one of them being the bomber that sank the *Lancastria*), making a total of 155. Hilly brought his personal score up to 17. Having been the first Fighter Squadron in France, No. 1 was the last but one to leave; 73 Squadron left fifteen minutes later.

In parenthesis, I should mention that " Moses," our interpreter, put up a very good show at this stage. He was ordered by the French authorities, in common with all the other Frenchmen attached to British units, to report to a depôt in Nantes. Rightly suspecting that the idea was to keep him in France, he disregarded his instructions and went down to the aerodrome dressed in overalls. Having unsuccessfully tried to get on to several crowded machines bound for England, he eventually found a Bristol " Bombay " (twin-engined bomber-transport) with a broken tail-wheel and damaged tail-unit, that was being left on the aerodrome. He persuaded a couple of R.A.F. N.C.O.'s to start the engines, and then flew the thing

to England with 15 troops aboard. He is now a
fighter pilot serving with the R.A.F., with six victories
already to his credit.

I myself left Châteaudun by air in a mail-plane (a
D.H. Rapide) on June 13th (the Germans entered
Paris on June 14th, and I learnt later, much to my
sorrow, that Dr. de Martell shot himself as they did
so). We took off in showery weather, circling the
bomb-pitted aerodrome with its destroyed hangars
and French aircraft blown on to their backs, and then
headed north-west for Normandy. Great black storm
clouds were rolling across the sky, and I hoped no
enemy fighters would pop round them, for we had no
armament. Below us, now in rainy shadow, now in
mottled sunlight, we could see the thousands and thousands of refugees stretched across the green countryside
like dirty white ribbons. From every town and every
village rose the crooked columns of smoke that betold
bombing, and now and then we would catch sight of a
stationary train. I had a camera with me, and no
doubt could have got some good pictures; but one
somehow felt it was not the moment, just as one
shrinks from taking pictures of a tragic accident.

Since my wound I had had an incredible capacity for
sleep, and I slept now. I awoke over the Channel
Islands; they were bathed in sunlight and stood out
very clearly in a smooth sea. Soon we were crossing
the Dorset coast; and as I looked down on the calm
and peaceful English countryside, the smoke curling,
not from bombed villages, but from lazy little cottage
chimneys, I saw a game of cricket in progress on a
village pitch. After the poor war-torn France I had
just seen in its death agony, I was seized with a sudden
disgust and revulsion at this smug insular contented-
ness and frivolity that England seemed to be enjoying
behind her sea barrier. I thought a few bombs would
wake those cricketers up, and that they wouldn't be
long in coming, either.

As we glided down on to Hendon aerodrome, my
feelings were so mixed that I had difficulty in con-

trolling them. I cannot describe them very well, and they don't really matter much anyway. I suppose it was a culmination of emotion that brought the tears to my eyes—something to do with the things I had done and seen, perhaps, with the friends I had left, and the almost unbelievable fact that I was home.

Well, as everyone knows, the Luftwaffe came to England. Many of us who fought in France were unable, through wounds or because we were doing other jobs, to take part in the Battle of Britain. But even so, and even though the Battle of France was lost, we like to think we had something to do with the saving of this Island. We like to think that we gave the Luftwaffe a little bit of a shaking up when we took the first shock in May, 1940. We like to think, too, that our experience helped the British Fighter Squadrons to inflict its first defeat on the Luftwaffe in August and September, 1940.

But that is another story.